THE CHURCH IN RUINS

FOUNDATIONS FOR THE FUTURE

Dr. William Crabb & Jeff Jernigan

NAVPRESS ◐
A MINISTRY OF THE NAVIGATORS
P.O. BOX 35001, COLORADO SPRINGS, COLORADO 80935

The Navigators is an international Christian
organization. Jesus Christ gave His followers
the Great Commission to go and make disciples
(Matthew 28:19). The aim of The Navigators is
to help fulfill that commission by multiplying
laborers for Christ in every nation.

NavPress is the publishing ministry of The Navigators. NavPress publications are tools to help
Christians grow. Although publications alone cannot make disciples or change lives, they can help
believers learn biblical discipleship, and apply
what they learn to their lives and ministries.

Cover illustration: Jeff Lauwers

Printed in the United States of America

FOR A FREE CATALOG OF
NAVPRESS BOOKS & BIBLE STUDIES,
CALL TOLL FREE 1-800-366-7788 (USA)
or 1-416-499-4615 (CANADA)

Contents

Authors

Dr. Bill Crabb served in the Air Force for twenty years, then retired in 1981 with the rank of lieutenant colonel. Toward the end of his military career, his interests shifted to seriously studying the Bible in order to understand God's plan for people. He acquired two master's degrees and a doctorate in counselor education, then left the Air Force to begin practicing as a licensed counselor.

Bill was a professor of counseling at Columbia Biblical Seminary for seven years while carrying on his private practice. He moved to Colorado Springs in 1989 and established Biblical Lifestyle Ministries with his associate, Brent Curtis. Just a week after finishing his work on *The Church in Ruins*, Bill died in an airplane crash. He left a wife, Phoebe, and two grown children, Caryn and Curtis.

Jeff Jernigan is a USMC Vietnam veteran who met Christ while in the military. His background includes social psychology, electrical engineering, and theology, and his professional experience includes engineering and human resource management. As members of the local church, Jeff and his wife, Diann, have been champions of the layperson for more than seventeen years, mobilizing and equipping men and women for a lifetime of laboring.

Jeff is currently co-founder and part owner of Peopleworks International, Inc., an international association of change consultants—leaders in the art and science of developing people and organizations. Jeff is also Vice President for U.S. Ministry for The Navigators. He and Diann live in Colorado Springs with their three children, Michael, Julia, and Daniel.

This book is for Phoebe, Caryn, and Curtis,

As well as for Diann,
Michael, Julia, and Daniel.

And finally, for Bill.
Everyone deserves a friend like Bill.
Few ever have them.

Acknowledgments

Bill often mentioned the help and counsel of his father, Lawrence J. Crabb, in preparing his materials for the book. Dr. Larry Crabb, Bill's brother, was a faithful friend and mentor through the process as well. On Bill's behalf, I thank you both. I want to thank Karen Hinckley, the perfect editor, for her patience and diligence in bringing her personality and expertise to bear in such a marvelous way. I am indebted as well to Janet Hock, my researcher and teacher. And to Jeanne Conder, my assistant and friend, I am especially grateful for her labors. Many more have knowingly and unknowingly influenced and helped this book along. For all of you, I thank God.

Foreword

Every person is confronted by the need to find something that makes life worth living. Parents whose dreams for their children are shattered, spouses who are deserted, hard workers who lose their jobs, health-conscious joggers who develop cancer, pastors whose congregations stubbornly don't respond, happy people who drift into black holes of depression—everyone has reason, at some point in life, to wonder why getting up in the morning is worth the effort.

The yearning for meaning, it must be said, is not selfish, nor is it a virtue. It simply *is*—a relentless, inescapable element in human existence that demands a response.

Most of us manage to quiet the demand by arranging for enough material and personal comforts to maintain a cheery optimism about life, as a rather pleasant experience that eventually yields to an even better one. Bad things, *really* bad things, aren't expected to cloud the skies, but if they do, then we provide ourselves with compensating pleasures to seal off whatever horrible pain and maddening questions may be provoked by difficult times. The majority of us fall into this first group of people who cope with life by selfish denial.

A second group lets the bad things make them morbid: always defeated and cynical, never joyfully spontaneous, forever worrying and complaining about something, frantically looking for relief from any quarter, or more commonly, bitterly resigning themselves to unavoidable misery (and feeling self-righteous about their heroic endurance). These are folks whose hearts and minds have never been penetrated with good news of any kind.

Then there is a third group of people who face the painful reality that they long for a level of meaning that is not easily felt. They admit, not proudly, that life hurts, that even their most comfortable moments don't feel like home, that relating with integrity to people holds the only hope of satisfying their thirst for a good reason to crawl out of bed, that relating with integrity is simply impossible without a vital relationship with God.

Three groups of people—shallow, morbid, and godly.

With disturbing accuracy, *The Church in Ruins* tells us that our modern churches, even some of the successful ones, are filled with folks from the first two groups. And worse, too many churches parade the characteristics of shallow people as commendable, and dismiss morbid folks as worthy only of a contemptuous sneer. And the few who are pursuing godliness without pretending that they always know how to do it are shamed as divisive and weak.

The message of this book is a hard one. I felt two reactions as I read it. First, if things are really bad enough to justify the title of the book (and I think they are), then I might as well spend more time playing golf. Why bother patching up walls that have already crumbled?

Second, I felt hopeful. There is something wonderfully relieving about facing things as they really are, no matter how bad, if you believe they could improve. And the authors of *The Church in Ruins* are hopeful. Notice the subtitle: *Foundations for the Future*. This is a realistically optimistic book. My second reaction was the stronger one. The first reaction was healthy because it made me more strongly value the second.

I have devoted my life to understanding how people can change into more of what God designed us to be. As I have realized some of the obstacles in the way of real change, my conviction has grown that nothing less than the power of God operating through human community can move us along the path. This book should be read by everyone who believes that local churches have unique resources for dealing with the real issues in people's lives and who realize that preaching to people who are not in vital relationship to one another greatly reduces the power of the pulpit.

Writing the foreword for this book has brought up a strange mixture of joy and sadness within me. It has been both deeply satisfying and intensely painful. One of the authors—Dr. William Crabb—is my brother. He was killed in an airplane crash one week after he completed the manuscript, and I am writing the foreword two months after his death.

Time is making me more aware of his absence. I thought it would be otherwise. Tears are welling up within me even as I write these words. But gratefully, along with tears, I have sensed through reading this book a deepened respect for the wisdom and the passion with which Bill thought about the things of God, especially the local church. It feeds my soul to realize that Bill believed what he said.

Bill's close friend and brother by conviction, Jeff Jernigan, co-authored the book. Together, they have written a book that our generation of success-oriented, performance-pressured, relationally distant Christians needs to hear. It radiates hope and encouragement!

I'm confident the message still matters to Bill, more now than before his death, because now he sees things from the perspective of a man who has seen Jesus—and actually talked with Him. And our Lord died to make it possible for us to relate to Him and to others with a love that can handle the way things really are. I believe this book reflects His heart for His people.

The Church in Ruins is an important book, one that has the potential to restore our churches to the redemptive community they were designed to be. May God use this book to help us all find the liberating reality of Christ in the midst of an otherwise intolerable life and to enable us to live out that reality by rebuilding ruined churches into loving communities.

—LARRY CRABB

PART ONE
THINGS
AS THEY ARE

1

Shrubs and Hedges

S am is on the way to "making it" in life. In his early forties,
living in the suburbs with his wife and two children, he
enjoys the benefits of dual incomes, two cars, Little League
baseball, block parties, and a growing collection of middle class
toys. For a long time, Sam had no spiritual dimension to his
life. "In God We Trust" on the coins in his pocket about said
it all. Though his parents had never set foot in a church, Sam
was willing to acknowledge that God was somewhere. After
all, Americans were "One Nation Under God." It really didn't
matter who God was as long as He didn't interfere.

During the course of a two-year relationship, a friend
introduced Sam to Jesus Christ and the "book of relationships" (this is how the Bible was first introduced to Sam). Sam
became a believer, as did his wife and children. Eventually, Sam
requested that their friend/pastor baptize them.

All of Sam's neighbors and coworkers were invited to his
baptism, which was held in his backyard swimming pool. Food
was laid out on card tables, and a keg of beer was provided
for the guests. Before Sam went under, he shared the stirring
story of his pilgrimage, how he came to be a follower of Christ.

Then, to a rousing toast of raised mugs, he entered the pool with the pastor.

The onlookers found Sam's new faith attractive, and the afternoon's activities seemed to unlock deep wells of spiritual curiosity in several of the guests. The pastor plans to follow up on these opportunities, taking Sam along for his own spiritual development. The pastor does not plan to immediately involve Sam's family in his church, or relate the details of Sam's baptism to the congregation.

❖ ❖ ❖

Two elders really got into it during this month's session meeting. Fred (sixty-two years old), finally fed up with Jerry's (thirty-three) attitude, yelled, "Jerry, I have had it with you! You are too committed to your own opinions, always concerned for the individual. What about the Body? What about the rest of us? I think your perspectives are just too selfish!"

Jerry expressed his long-repressed resentment. "Well, I'm glad you brought the matter up. Your attitude has stuck in my craw for a long time. You don't belong on this board. You're a spineless wimp who cops out to the party line every time a decision comes to a vote! I don't think you have ever had an opinion of your own. This session doesn't need 'company' men!"

❖ ❖ ❖

Amanda grew up in the church. As a teenager, she saw her parents struggling with the same issues as the parents of her friends who had nothing to do with the church. It didn't seem to her that the church made a difference at all in resolving financial difficulties, protecting the children from the abuse they suffered, or delivering parents from inevitable, messy divorces. God didn't seem to make any difference in the pain they experienced.

By the time Amanda left for college, she thought of God as a disinterested third party, an onlooker uninvolved in a world

He may have created. She tried church for a while but found the same empty (for her) rituals, the same uninteresting music, the same boring appeals for money she remembered from home. No one expressed concern for the problems she faced, or interest in the things that really motivated her. The singles pastor even told Amanda, when she shared her excitement about being involved in a campus organization that addressed environmental issues, that membership in the singles fellowship would have to be on his terms. And he saw no room for divided commitments in the midst of a busy schedule of activities.

Amanda hasn't stepped foot in any church since that conversation.

✛ ✛ ✛

Bill and Ginger visited our church one Sunday. As business acquaintances, they had expressed an interest in getting to know us better. With no children of their own yet, time around our family seemed to really encourage the relationship and disarm them regarding our "religious beliefs."

After church, we took them to lunch and expressed interest in their reaction. In our opinion, the sermon that morning had been excellent! Right from the Bible, with great exegesis, the preacher had woven a picture of God's love for each of us by using the story of David's failure with Bathsheba. Plenty of good stuff to identify with and be encouraged by, we thought. Sunday school had been planned by God. A new quarter was starting and various members of the class volunteered their testimonies to help break the ice for the new class. The gospel was especially clear, but with no embarrassing hard sell for the newcomers. During the half-hour fellowship between the worship service and Sunday school Ginger enjoyed her favorite doughnuts, and Bill met two other business acquaintances. Friendly, animated conversation resulted. After church, the pastor spent a few extra minutes with us making this couple feel welcome and affirming our role in the church. We could not have orchestrated a better morning for them! Or so we thought!

"Would you like to visit again?" we asked. Without hesitation, Bill said no. My surprise must have been obvious, for he offered an explanation without prompting. "You certainly have a great church there, and we enjoyed meeting all those nice people. But I could never get over the feeling like I was at my wife's high school reunion."

"What do you mean?" I asked.

"Well, my wife and I didn't go to the same high school. When I went with her to their ten-year reunion, I met a lot of nice people who certainly accepted me, but I never shed the feeling of being an outsider all night. They were reminiscing about memories I didn't have, sharing feelings I haven't experienced, laughing together about events I never participated in. Many of them had hung together since high school and obviously felt uncomfortable when I joined their group.

"Your preacher seemed to be a nice enough guy, but he just isn't where I'm at. For instance, I have an employee who borders on being lazy, just enough to frustrate me. I was kind of hoping something he'd share from the Bible would tell me how to deal with that. Then there were all those words he used that just don't compute."

"Like what?" I asked, beginning to feel a little defensive.

"He kept talking about David's 'sin.' I finally figured out that what he called sin, I call fun. And I never did figure out what he meant by 'grace' or 'atonement' or 'repentance.' I thought I knew what those words meant until he started hanging all this spiritual stuff all over them. I almost asked the preacher on the way out, 'If God is so loving, how come He zapped David's kid just for this fling with the chick next door?' but I figured I wouldn't understand his answer anyway."

Ginger volunteered that she felt the folks that shared in the class were really into themselves.

"What do you mean?" I asked.

"Well," she paused, "they seemed only interested in what Jesus did for them—not just this salvation stuff but all the goodies they want. Sounds like this Jesus is some sort of Aladdin's Lamp. It really bugged me. On the way to the church, we passed the public housing project my 'Food for the Hungry' group is involved in. The flyer we got coming into the church that describes what the church is doing doesn't mention a single thing that really touches people who don't belong to this church. And the housing project is just two blocks away!"

Four Challenges to the Church

These true stories reflect growing realities in the church today. The pastor doesn't want to involve Sam's family in his church yet because he knows from experience that the few families that have joined as a result of a decision for Christ are quickly cut off from their nonChristian friends. As the family becomes insulated by their new Christian environment from the lost world, the pastor's opportunities for real evangelism in the community will quickly come to an end.

This decision to keep Sam on his own turf frustrates the pastor because he feels pressure (from himself, the denomination, and perceived from the Lord) for his church to grow. He knows most of his church growth has come from other Christians—those wooed away from other congregations, new in town, or children of families already in the church—not the lost in the community. Sam is an ideal chance for this pastor to really do the Great Commission in his own backyard instead of in some foreign country. Why? Because Sam's natural lines of relationship give access to the lost, and his testimony makes sense to them.

But there is a catch. The deacons would probably let the pastor work with Sam outside the church for a time, especially if there were results. But they would never condone the beer.

"True, it will have to go," the pastor feels. "Right now, though, it is a minor issue compared to other needs in Sam's life."

Fred and Jerry in the second illustration are both staunch Presbyterians, but they come from different eras in American society. Fred grew up in a time that emphasized community; a person shared and sacrificed personal desires for the benefit of the group. Jerry, a "baby boomer" rather than part of the "establishment," grew up in different times. Politics, the economy, and other influences have so reshaped American society that Jerry's perspective on life is much more individualistic. He cares about developing a person's spiritual gifts to maximize his or her contribution to the Body. Jerry believes strongly that as individuals are enabled to serve, the team functions better.

Fred and Jerry are both committed Christians and, in this case, further discussion reveals that their motivations are understandable. However, they are driven by different value systems. Different isn't always wrong. The problem lies in a subtle assumption that unity requires uniformity. In reality, the diversity pictured for the Body of Christ in 1 Corinthians 12–14 guarantees a mosaic in our congregations! In the United States today, there are at least four different sets of age-related value systems, and social, economic, and geographic groupings guarantee even more diversity.

Most of the approaches to ministry that the North American institutional church currently uses emerged from the earliest of these age-related value systems (represented by Fred). The methodology, programs, and systems of the church reflect the cultural assumptions of this system. But the more unlike Fred his audience is, the less they will see the church as relevant. Amanda in our third illustration is reacting to perceived irrelevance. Her church is relevant to some, but not to her peers (who will soon statistically outnumber her forbears). Amanda needs a relational ministry that keeps people from becoming projects. For her, people are the key, not programs. She will judge the relevance of religion by its ability to address, from her perspective and experience, the problems of her day in ways that genuinely help. If her generation is going to own and live the gospel for itself, that gospel needs to be communicated in terms that are *receiver-oriented* (sensitive to the hearer's needs and abilities) as opposed to *messenger-oriented* (tied to the speaker's comfort).

Finally, Bill and Ginger represent a growing number of unreached Americans. The churched (those saved and lost people who attend church somewhat regularly) and unchurched (those saved and lost who don't attend church but who have some Christian background) at least have a religious heritage—some exposure to the message of the church and some common spiritual concepts that allow mutual understanding. But the unreached, now a growing segment of our population, lack that religious heritage. Like Sam's family, Bill and Ginger are a third generation that has never set foot in a church or had any exposure to religion in a formal way. To them, Christianity is a different culture; even though we use the same words, Christians speak a different language.

Out of Touch

America's accelerating social change challenges the church's relevance. Traditionalism, conflicting values (like Fred's and Jerry's), institutional ministry, and changes in how various subcultures define themselves are making it increasingly hard for us to reach the lost and meaningfully serve the saved. But doing so are also the church's greatest opportunities.

Many research organizations, both secular and religious, have documented that numerical church growth is stagnating and the church is more and more cut off from society. Periodicals feature articles that describe how the church is less and less involved redemptively in American life. Christian authors are focusing attention on the church's growing irrelevance outside the confines of its own congregations. What is it that these scholars and lay people alike see, and why is it so alarming? Simply put: *The church today is out of touch.*

The shift from a focus on community in society to a focus on the individual has closed certain opportunities for communicating the gospel and created new ones. Methodologies that focus on society's "windows" (open lines of communication) must adjust to new windows. The church must recognize that the relationship between the individual and society is continually changing. The establishment (age forty-four and up), baby boomers (twenty-five to forty-three), and baby busters (twenty-four and under) have different values, different perceived needs, and very different perspectives on life and reality. American society is far less homogeneous than it may have once appeared to be. An approach to ministry that assumes little or no change in the audience is guaranteed to become irrelevant. Sooner or later, the audience will move away from the assumptions behind the method. Therefore, we need what I call a *missiological* approach to ministry—one bound not by methods, but only by our biblical mission. Such an approach can be continually relevant without compromising biblical truth. It will require a new philosophy of leadership and ministry in the church—vital institutional change from within.

I had an engaging conversation with a spiritually curious fellow passenger on an airline flight that forcibly reminded me why we must emphasize the person instead of method or program. In the course of our chat he showed interest in the gospel, so I began to share with him, using a method I learned in a popular evangelism training course.

The illustrations did not communicate. Repeatedly, my "audience" asked questions about terminology and unfamiliar concepts. Paul was interested in how the gospel affected my life, not in someone else's story or concepts. He was thirty-three, divorced, a successful businessman, and an unreached baby boomer. His spiritual curiosity was genuine, sprinkled with questions not phrased as objections but certainly thoughtful.

So I switched to another approach. "Paul, I have a brief picture I can draw that may explain further what I am trying to say." I drew another popular witnessing tool from my arsenal. As the picture on the notebook paper between us grew, so did Paul's confusion. Words like *sin, wages, judgment,* and *eternal life* found no resonance in his thinking. Unlike the unchurched, who have a religious heritage to draw from, three generations of his family had never seen the inside of a church. Paul, like a growing number in this country, had no background in his thinking to help him understand the gospel.

When we came to the concept of grace in Ephesians 2:8-9, he stopped me in frustration. Pulling from his briefcase a small paperback dictionary, Paul looked up the word. We found several secular definitions that were acceptable, and the conversation continued with more understanding.

I learned several things from this experience. First, I discovered that it is dangerous to assume everyone approaches the gospel message with the same background, experience, or heritage. Each audience has traits that may aid or hinder understanding. Most methods for communicating scriptural truth are developed using certain social examples. To audiences not focused on the same or related examples, the message will be ineffective, even to the point of irrelevance.

The church is out of touch with more than just value systems. It is also ignoring a host of related, rapidly changing social factors. Dual-career households, single parenting, divorce, and alternate lifestyles are changing the nuclear family. Most Americans live in urban settings, a radical shift from just twenty years ago. But most pastoral training assumes a philosophy of education developed in rural settings. (Some important elements of a rural ethic are status quo, harmony, smallness, and resistance to change. By contrast, the urban ethic stresses conflict, bigness, and a demand for change.) Ethnicity is on the increase.

Asians and Hispanics will be larger subcultures than African Americans in this country in the next fifty years. In fact, white Americans will be a minority in many places. The church is faced with adapting to unprecedented diversity.

Joseph, an ethnic pastor, commented recently on the changes in his own ministry. Even the barber shop has changed. The barber doesn't talk about the fights or football. A budding author, he talks about poetry. Nobody reads the magazines as they wait. They sit silently or chat about who is living with whom. The free literature comes from cults or the nearby denominational church, which distributes tracts written by whites for whites. "Who," Joseph wanted to know, "is taking into consideration the multiethnic, urban nature of our communities?"

God's Part, Our Part

We must realize that getting back in touch isn't all up to us. Somewhere along the line, room must be made for God to work. Much of what the church does these days leaves out the Holy Spirit. We have become overly skilled at making our organizations run, so we have little need for the intervening, life-changing power of prayer.

A Chinese professor studying in this country cut my heart to the quick one afternoon with a simple observation. He was a Christian who had been allowed to leave Communist China for a period of study. I was fascinated by his testimony. I asked Chew for observations from his travels in America regarding the church. He had two: "Whole families in my city can live off what you throw away," and "It is amazing what you can accomplish without the Holy Spirit."

Our expertise in ministry provides success (numbers, programs) without supernatural involvement. The church is big business. But a missiological approach to ministry will accomplish nothing if it is not sanctified by the Word of God and prayer, exemplified by a humbled life, empowered by the Holy

Spirit, and built on the gifts and calling of the average believer.

Now, about shrubs and hedges. The feeling you get trying to relate the title of this chapter to the contents is the same feeling those outside the church get trying to relate the message of the church to their lives. There doesn't appear to be any connection.

A revealing dialogue took place recently at a Presidential Prayer Breakfast in Washington, D.C. Many dignitaries from the United States and abroad were there representing government, business, and industry. It was a marvelous opportunity for Christian witness and building relationships with a redemptive focus. But a careful observer would have noticed that words like *Bible* and *Christian* quickly ended conversations rather then enhanced them. In marked contrast, those talking about being "followers of Jesus" and reading the "Book of Relationships" were able to tap deep wells of spiritual need and curiosity. Those conversations were animated. Yet why this change in attitude due simply to terminology?

It is more than a communication gap. Different philosophies and values are involved. Christianity in America has become its own subculture with all the attendant problems of "doing business" cross-culturally. We even have our own language. To the unchurched and the unreached, Christian terminology carries certain baggage. It represents a world view that in their experience has included paternalism, ethnocentrism, legalism, conformity, and even dishonesty and immorality. Christianity is just another culture with its own norms and values, which are inherently no better or worse than those of the listening culture.

The church must contextualize its presence in society if it is to grow in relevance, sustain health, and hold forth the Word in truth and integrity. Otherwise, we might as well be talking about shrubs and hedges.

2

Changing Spots

The church is caught in a tension. Our society is changing; economic, business, and political realities are in constant flux. As a people, we feel this pressure ceaselessly. Yet as individuals we resist change, feeling more secure with a stable environment. This constant pressure from society to change and the tendency for individuals to resist change create tension.

Humans generally respond to such pressure either by adapting or by creating an artificial environment around them that does not require adaptation. Accordingly, the church in North America has tended to respond in two directions. Either it has compromised its authority and become too secular, or it has become insular and irrelevant, ignoring changing social realities.

Jesus modeled for us a middle ground. He was relevant continuously but without compromise. Jesus was a Jew. He was raised in Judaism. The Hebrew culture of the first century was His context. Sometimes that simple reality escapes us. *Context* is what gives meaning to words and brings understanding to events. The message of Christ's life communicated clearly to those who shared His context. For those who did not share His context, He chose to modify His actions and change His words in order to fit the message more clearly to the hearers' heritage, language, customs—their context. The gospel is simple enough that the message can be made contextual without compromising the truth. It requires, however, that the messenger recognize the differences between his culture and the receiving culture and adapt accordingly.

The Problem with Methods

Many recognize this truth, but few see its implications. Most attempts to contextualize ministry focus on changing methods and activities, not on changing the philosophy of the messenger. Consequently, ministry—to the saved and lost alike—becomes oriented to methods or programs. When one approach fails, it is replaced by a new activity, one that comes from the same methodological approach and will soon be revealed as equally irrelevant. Even when activities are tailored to a particular audience, if there is no fundamental shift in the mindset behind the ministry, it, too, will fail.

A missiological approach to ministry requires different values, assumptions, and beliefs than does an institutionally supported, program-centered, method-focused approach. The messenger changes in thinking and action (*conceptual* and *practical philosophy*) as he or she becomes a cross-boundary missionary to America.

A well-meaning minister wrote at length to me recently describing his ministry. Frustrated for some time about evangelism, he recognized the difference between himself and his audience, and began to question some of his institutionalized assumptions about ministry. His need to identify with his audience was clear, but his attempts to contextualize ministry revealed a lack of understanding of what it really means to put yourself and the gospel in someone else's context.

He wrote, "My wife, Jane, and I were constantly seeking

ways to minister to the unbeliever. We had conducted a divorce recovery group and tried many other avenues of ministries such as a game night, special meals, visitation with senior citizens and taking food to the ill. . . . One-on-one we could give much spiritual input, but we were in the cultivating stage of bringing them to the point where they would want to take part in [a group Bible study]."

Obviously, this minister has a heart for these people and is trying to meet needs in ways that will provide spiritual opportunities. However, his approach is activity-centered and assumes the social framework of his own lifestyle and past ministry experience. His audience, as the letter went on to demonstrate, wants relationships, not meetings. The one thing he is doing that seems to work (one-on-one contact) he views as a step toward another activity, not a relational opportunity to expand ministry itself.

The letter described an incident when a man with a beer in hand dropped into a Bible study for Christians. It was soon obvious that this person was not there for the Bible study. He came because he was hurting and did not want to sit alone in his apartment. He was uncomfortable about joining the group because of the beer in his hand. A few in the group were equally uncomfortable. Fortunately, the minister communicated acceptance, not necessarily approval, and the visitor sat with them for a while.

Few people are recruited this way. How often does an unbeliever wander into the foreign territory of a Bible study? Seldom. Why? It seems to be the nature of humans to prefer people and settings that reflect values and customs they share. White, professional, secular, middle-aged men feel most comfortable in familiar surroundings doing and discussing the kinds of things other white, professional, secular, middle-aged men enjoy. Drop them into a black, feminine, or blue-collar environment, and watch them struggle with feeling like aliens.

That's what happened to secular Bill and Ginger when I (Jeff) dropped them into Christian culture. It is also what happened to the young man with the beer; he couldn't wait to get back to a setting where he knew the rules, understood the language, and shared the beliefs and values.

But most evangelism strategies emphasize inviting or attracting someone to an activity. If that activity is culturally "Christian"—such as a Bible study, a rally, a Christian speaker or concert—we can expect substantial resistance from our unbelieving friends. Unless they are the kind of people who enjoy being out of their depth in foreign cultures, they will probably either decline our invitation or attend our activity with all of their defenses up.

"Come-to" strategies will not generally attract those we want to reach in the relationally impoverished America of today. An emotionally secure person is not afraid to venture into strange social situations, but a person who can barely manage relationships with people like himself will flee from the unknown. A generation raised on divorce is not equipped to come to us. Therefore, we must develop "go-to" approaches to ministry that bring us alongside those we would minister to. *We* have to be the secure ones willing to venture into social situations that reflect values we deplore.

The letter continued: "This young person was struggling with the fact that he was not being praised every time he performed the duties of his job. He needed to see that when we do as we are ordered, we have not gone the second mile." A lesson from Luke 17:7-10 on the unworthy servant followed. In his favor, this minister unashamedly applied the Word of God. It is the Word and the Spirit of God that have power (Romans 1:16-17), not the persuasive words of men. There is no need to hide the Word in embarrassed statements of deferral. This minister also recognized the flaw in his visitor's values about work and its rewards.

But the minister used Scripture to point out what was wrong with the young man's attitude, rather than to encourage him with what could be different and give him hope for the future. This was a fatal mistake. The gospel is a message of hope, not condemnation. The instruction this young man received was focused on correcting his behavior, not on dealing with underlying motivation. The answer this young man endured came from the minister's generation.

What the young man really needed went far deeper than an adjusted attitude about reward in the workplace. The minister was trying to help his visitor come to grips with a symptom, when Christ died to set him free from the disease. The young man never came back. He saw only condemnation and missed the hope that comes from relational involvement.

This minister, specializing in evangelism, ended his letter enthusiastically. They are seeing results from the use of these activities in nontraditional settings (they don't meet in a church). But in reality, his approach to ministry is very traditional. The results are primarily among the saved, with little or no impact outside God's family. Institutional methodology creates a form or activity, invites or attracts people to come, exposes the audience to the Word (often in accusatory fashion) and puts the responsibility for success or failure on the program, not people.

There is a wise proverb for such oft-unrecognized patterns: If it walks like a duck, sounds like a duck, and looks like a duck—it must be a duck. Despite a sincere desire to reach the unreached, this minister was irrelevant and ineffective.

What We Say and What We Do

It isn't only individuals like this man who think they understand how to make their ministries relevant when the gap between what they say and what they do is huge. Entire organizations can suffer from this apparent blindness.

In affirming the mandate for world evangelization, a major denomination recently published its commitment in this way: "Philosophy of Missions? Stated in two words it is, 'Jesus Christ.' . . . The ultimate method of missions is to wrap life around the gospel and live it out." This sounds very incarnational, very relational, very relevant. The official position goes on to say that the denomination has demonstrated its belief that local congregations are the basic and authoritative element in the shared life as a denomination. This placing of responsibility on the local congregation for missions (as opposed to the denominational structure) and the emphasis on modeling the message sound very contextual. Few would disagree with the importance of the local church and a relevant testimony backing up the proclamation of the gospel.

However, a careful look at the assumptions behind these statements reveals something else altogether. The official commitment to reaching the lost is to concentrate on evangelism that results in churches. As these churches multiply, they are encouraged to relate to each other and to express their unique (denominational) concept in their own ways. Any approach to reaching the lost that is not an integral part of church growth or church planting is not officially sanctioned, not a part of the denominational strategy.

Efforts to reach the lost are confined to boundaries. Those boundaries come not from biblical absolutes, but from strategies designed to reproduce forms the denomination favors. And those forms also are not biblical absolutes, but have merely evolved to suit a single culture. Relevant to some, these ministries will exclude many others—indeed, most others.

Pastoral training in this denomination holds up a similarly restricted model of a missions-minded person. A limited vocabulary is suggested; always and only talk about one subject, Jesus, while doing evangelism. (Evangelism is viewed as an activity, an event, not a process.) Other conversations are to be avoided. Lifestyle is to be equally focused; have nothing to do with the world at all. This rule limits involvement with the lost to only activities associated with evangelism. Ministry is narrowly defined; everything we do should be directly related to spreading the gospel by proclamation.

The dichotomy between the stated conceptual philosophy, which appears to encourage contextualization of ministry, and the actual philosophy taught in seminaries and practiced in the church is clear. Regardless of position statements to the contrary, what is practiced is an institutional, activity-oriented, methodological approach to ministry. The approach assumes that America is a mono-cultural audience; it is not. There are major social groups to which this approach is totally irrelevant.

The "Average" American

Before we look at these different groups, let's consider something. The leopard needs to change its spots. Becoming a striped tiger, a maned lion—whatever—depends on the audience, not the institution. If God has sent us to do a job, we do it in whatever way works best and honors Him, not in the way most comfortable for us. Paul had this in mind when he described his desire to become all things to all people (1 Corinthians 9:22). Ministry forms should be receiver-oriented ("What serves the other person?"), not messenger-oriented ("What serves me?").

But how can institutions change without corrupting the message or self-destructing? The process begins with understanding the audience.

My youngest son developed an earache while on vacation on Cape Cod. The day before we were to fly home, we took him to a local hospital because the infection wasn't clearing up. While sitting in the hospital waiting room, I asked a fellow vacationer, in the context of a conversation we struck up, if he could describe the "average American." Not surprisingly, he described someone not unlike himself. I tried it again the next day on the airplane and again in the office when I returned to work, with identical results. Few seem to really be in touch with the major shifts occurring in our society, though they do seem relatively in touch with their own social circles. For the church, this is dangerous if all people see is their own kind.

Those I talked to would be surprised to learn the average American is a thirty-two-year-old single woman. Though she hasn't been to church in the past week, she believes in God and life after death but has not had a religious awakening. A Protestant, she has been married once and has one child. She probably works in a technical, sales, or administrative job. As fast as she makes money, it gets spent. None of the people I talked with described the average American in those terms, but viewing themselves as the average American gave a good description of their current situation.

It can get confusing. North America in general is currently focused on the individual. There is an emphasis on duty to self over others. Concern for rights overshadows concern with responsibility. Anxiety about the present supplants care for the future. Differences in people grab attention rather than shared commonalities. It can be expressed in the overt, selfish "meism" so many have written about, or in a subtle shift in focus away from altruism that is hard to notice.

There are approximate generational divisions as well. Those people who are the establishment (forty-four years and up) have been around the longest, have the most experience, and generally are cautious or conservative in their approach to life. Coming from a more communal period in American society, they have a naturally suspicious and skeptical view of younger, more individualistic generations.

Baby boomers (ages twenty-four to forty-three) thrive on diversity, insist on it. They have great zeal for change of the status quo. They desire to maximize an individual's potential, even demand it. Success is measured in materialistic quantifiers. They are eminently pragmatic; if it works, do it.

Baby busters (under age twenty-four) will be true Information Age people. They are not a transition group like the boomers (there are approximately 77 million baby boomers in a closed segment of American society). Instead, the buster outlook promises to hold sway and deepen as the years pass.

For the busters, right and wrong hold less importance. Whereas the establishment tends to define right and wrong in terms of some social or moral ethic, and boomers more in terms of what is good or bad for self, most busters have only shades of right; there are no wrongs.

The familial disruption (divorce, single parenting, abuse, etc.) appearing as problems in the boomers will be life patterns for busters. Later busters, responding to urbanization and the growing ethnicity of the United States, will shift further in social paradigm and face economic issues of class structure.

Each of these groups has among them the churched, unchurched, and unreached. Nearly 40 percent of our population fits in the unchurched and unreached categories. Also, most of the country lives in urban settings, metropolitan or suburban.

This shift in social ethic from community to individual, different driving value systems, and a lack of religious consensus in this country present unique challenges to ministry. And the diversity is increasing at an ever faster pace. Traditional evangelical methodology may reach and serve those with a religious heritage, but is far less effective in reaching others. Some report that the population of the church in North America has remained relatively constant over the last thirty years. But the population in this country has not remained static. We are slowly being outnumbered.

A family I know illustrates well this social diversity. The oldest son is in his mid-forties, an establishment person whose first wife was an Asian national. The youngest son is in his mid-thirties, married to an Asian American, and is clearly an unreached boomer. The middle son, also a boomer, would be classified as unchurched, having a religious heritage that the youngest missed as a result of his parents' divorce in his teen years. A daughter, who married Hispanic nationals twice, is a churched boomer. All of their children are busters. That is, truth for these kids is relative. There are no rights or wrongs. But unlike the humanism we are familiar with that denies the existence of God, they admit to a spiritual dimension consisting of many gods.

These families come from rural and urban backgrounds, have four ethnic groups represented, reflect three age-related value systems, have experienced four divorces, have a sustained marriage of over twenty years in their midst, have lived through a communal-to-individual shift in our culture, and are raising nine children in an environment with which their parents and grandparents cannot identify. This kind of diversity is commonplace in most communities and congregations, and presents unique challenges to evangelism and discipleship.

My wife and I were sobered by the pace of change in a recent course we took together. We had enrolled in a parenting class offered by a local college through our children's school district. In our family, there is a nine-year span separating our oldest in college from his youngest sibling, a brother in junior high, with a sister in between. We learned that what our youngest faces in school now is radically different from the issues faced by our oldest when he was in junior high. It was not, as our earlier parenting experience would suggest, discipline problems or drugs reaching children earlier in the school system. Latchkey kids, concepts of authority, security and significance issues associated with single parenting all have changed the junior high student's world. How children think, how they conceptualize reality (their world view) is very different. As a result of this small snapshot of a quickly changing world, we adjusted some of our parenting strategies.

Process, Not Program

Contextualization is more than adaptation. It is a process, not a program, of becoming a part of the audience to be reached. It requires crossing social and cultural boundaries without compromise to Scripture. Contextualization is continual, not something achieved by following a formula or program. In addition to knowing the audience and its world view, contextualization requires a relevant philosophy of ministry in application.

It will take more than a program to reach Albert, a typical buster. New Age thinking—unfamiliar, awkward, and seemingly unreasonable—affects our children more than we are aware. Albert invited Christ into his life in elementary school. By his senior year in high school, Al decided Christianity was irrelevant. His church experience made Christianity look like manmade mythology. The appeal of the New Age was in its "realistic" approach in a rationalistic world.

The institutional church had no answers to Albert's social environment and pragmatic religious questions. Al felt he had complied with ritual but never had any faith belief. Now a member of the unchurched (lost, yet having a religious heritage), he integrated his Christian education with Eastern mysticism: Fallen man is simply out of tune with nature, not with a supreme deity. Eventually the bankruptcy of this philosophy led him to the Lord, but it was largely due to the faithfulness of God's pursuit, not the efforts of the church.

The problem with being too adaptive or too insular is losing touch with the audience or compromising Scripture by trying to relate inappropriately. Yet changing cultural norms demand that the church remain in touch if it is to nurture its constituency and reach the lost. In later chapters, we will explore just how this can be done.

3

A Future Illusion

B ob believed the Lord had called him into ministry. He was a very committed man sincerely wanting to be what he was called by God to be. So he resigned his employment and financial security and moved his wife and two children to a highly respected seminary to prepare for a life of service as a pastor at home or on the mission field.

Seminary was hard. In addition to the academic work, Bob worked part-time, and his wife accepted all the substitute teaching she could get to help with tuition, rent, and other necessities. Neither one talked about the hardships and lack of time together as a family, believing that upon graduation God would use them in an effective ministry.

Finally, the big day came. Bob received his Master of Divinity degree and was actively sought out by a growing, radiant church to be their senior pastor. Things seemed to fall into place so well that he was convinced God was strongly leading him and his family in this direction. Now in his early forties, he firmly believed he was finally where God wanted him.

As he moved to his first church, Bob thought back on his years at seminary and began to pray and plan how he would meet his new responsibilities. He had studied hard, graduated near the top of his class, and was complimented on his gifts as a preacher and teacher. As a former successful businessman, he had a measure of confidence as an administrator. As he left seminary, his briefcase was full of what he believed he needed to effectively pastor a church of committed believers. He had administrative experience, and his knowledge of Scripture definitely gave him a basis to answer questions and provide solutions to problems. God had prepared him for ministry!

A Harsh Reality

Bob's preaching initially seemed to have impact. His sermons were well received as he preached the gospel forcefully and, verse by verse, expounded the truth of God's Word. But as the months went by, he felt that his sermons weren't being as well received, and several people who came to see him about serious problems didn't come back. Knowing that ministry can sometimes be lonely and discouraging, he pressed on, preaching, teaching, administering, and counseling. He knew something was wrong but was unsure what it was or what to do about it.

One of the people Bob counseled was Ann, a single woman in her early thirties with a difficult background. Her natural parents were not married, and her father disappeared shortly after her birth. Her mother married several years later. As a result, beginning about age seven, Ann became the victim of physical and sexual abuse from her stepfather.

He drank frequently and was either physically abusive when angry or sexually aggressive when in a "loving" mood. As is typical of abused children, out of fear Ann had been silent as to what happened to her. Now an adult, she was very overweight, outwardly active in the church but inwardly doubting her salvation and questioning God as a loving Father. (The concept of a loving father was completely foreign to her experience.) When she went to her pastor, she was beginning to slowly back away from her active involvement in the church as her doubts about a loving God and her salvation grew.

Pete was the son of a highly successful businessman. He was well educated, had been made vice president of his father's business, and had made some excellent investments. He sang in the church choir, was a leader in the singles group, and seemed, at thirty-five, to have it made.

He came to Bob one day in tears over the facade he had maintained over the years. His life was empty; he resented his father for the pressure he felt to carry on the family business according to what he perceived as his father's impossible expectations. Worst of all, his involvement in and support of the church was superficial and not bringing about the prayed-for results. After all, didn't God promise to satisfy the desires of his heart if he was faithful? His job put him under constant pressure and was not personally rewarding. He worked hard, longing for his father's respect, which never seemed to come. Despite how busy and involved he was in the church, it never filled the void in his life as he had expected. Continual work, involvement, and prayer weren't producing what he longed for.

Bob fully believed that questions had answers and problems had solutions, and he went to the Bible to find them. He told Ann, accurately, that God loved her sufficiently to send His Son to die for her sins and make her His child. Now as an adult, she had a responsibility to follow Him, to remain active in the church, get involved in a weight loss program so she would have a better opportunity to date, and to forget the past and press on for her Savior.

Bob knew that for some reason his message to Ann wasn't sinking in. Was he teaching ineffectively? She seemed to be resistant and was ignoring God's truth. Why wasn't the truth of God's love transforming her life? Why did she cling to her obesity when clearly, losing weight would enhance her opportunity to date and find a lifetime partner? Was her problem rebellion? Maybe she wasn't even a Christian. Bob didn't know how he could help Ann.

Pete, on the other hand, seemed to respond very positively to Bob's teaching and suggestions. He increased his giving, resumed his interest in church activities, and on the surface, seemed to be going forward for Jesus Christ.

Bob was shocked when he was called to the hospital. Pete had unsuccessfully attempted suicide. What went wrong? Everything seemed so good on the surface.

If questions had answers and problems had solutions, where had Bob failed? The harsh reality was he didn't know how to help Ann or Pete. And even worse, other problems in his church were beginning to surface. Several parents had adolescent children who were sexually active and experimenting with drugs, and he felt responsible to provide answers to questions and solutions to problems. That was what he believed God had called him to do.

Repent, Perform, and Pay

Several years ago, an intelligent, well-read woman, who on the surface seemed to be in control of her life, made an insightful observation. She was becoming disillusioned with the church and said no matter where she turned, she always got the same answer: repent from your sinful patterns of behavior, join the church, witness, get your thoughts off yourself, get busy for God, and support the church financially. She and others like her (Ann and Pete) tried very hard. After all, doesn't the Apostle Paul exhort us to forget the past and strain forward for Jesus Christ? But Ann and Pete and *countless* others can't seem to forget the past. Their abuse, humiliations, and expectations seem to control their very being. They see few options.

The fact that they can't forget the past means to them

either that they haven't tried hard enough and that the Spirit of God won't work until they do their part (repent and perform at a sufficient level) or perhaps they believe they aren't even Christians. The memories are so painful, the anger is so real, the hopelessness growing. "God has clearly done His part; the problem must be me" is stated over and over by people like Ann and Pete. To them, the situation seems hopeless, and Bob's "encouragement" and confrontation seem to make matters worse. They just can't measure up.

Is Paul really telling us to forget the past in Philippians 3:13 where he says, "Forgetting what is behind and straining toward what is ahead"? Earlier in chapter 3, he talks about his past, his sinful zeal, his claim to righteousness by birth and law keeping. If he had forgotten them, why did he list his past failures and shortcomings?

It is because he is not telling us to forget the past. The issue is not going forward for God in order to blot out the memory of the past. Paul is asking us to become more and more aware of how we have sinfully learned to cope with the past, to face the ugly reality of our past, and not allow it to control our lives anymore. That's what Paul did. He saw how he was trying to cover sin by performance, and he was adamant in Romans 7 that it doesn't work.

When we try to cover the pain of our past and our despair in the present, we are living in denial in two ways. First, the past did happen, and the present felt pain is real. No amount of performance will ultimately help eliminate a painful past and present. They must be faced. Rather than performance, we need rich community to help one another by bearing burdens, weeping with those who weep, and entering into one another's joy. We need an atmosphere where sinful learned patterns of living can be safely exposed and a loving God's perspective can be learned.

Second, we are attempting to make our mask of denial so

rigid that everyone we meet sees us as strong, victorious Christians. In doing so, we are denying that the Body of Christ has a vital part in our process of coming to face reality under God's authority. We can't do it alone, and we are kidding ourselves when we try.

A New Perspective

Several years ago, I heard Chuck Swindoll say that a grief shared is half a grief. I believe he was saying that pain is not fixable, that not all questions have answers, and that not all problems have solutions. In other words, the Bible deals realistically with all questions and problems, but maybe the answers we want aren't the answers Scripture gives. Maybe God doesn't promise to end our pain while we are on earth.

Can Ann's past and her pain be blotted out? Can we find a biblical formula to make Pete's world work according to his perspective and expectations? The answer is an absolute NO!

Pastor Bob's advice and Chuck Swindoll's statement are based on two radically different and opposite perspectives about living in a fallen world. Bob was satisfied when Pete's outward expression masked an inward reality. Bob was frustrated when Ann didn't change her behavior to comply with "biblical" norms of behavior. But Ann was at least honest. She knew there was a deep chasm between facts and inward reality. Can we expect to "fix" a painful inward reality through biblical behavior?

Does the popular teaching "change your behavior and the feelings will follow" hold water? One of my students rephrased this teaching as "fake it until you make it." The trouble is that we don't make it, at least according to our expectations. We can't blot out the pain of the past. It can't and won't be fixed (no longer experienced) this side of Heaven. That is also a harsh reality. The past cannot be forgotten in that sense.

Furthermore, merely changing our behavior can increase

frustration when we fail to face what we are expecting (even secretly demanding) from God as a result of our "faithfulness." All too often we are really trying to make a deal with God: "If I'm good, Lord, You'll reward me by giving me what I want, right?" Then, when we behave rightly for a while, but our feelings or circumstances don't change, we feel God has cheated us. But He never agreed to the deal. We need to renew our mind, not just alter our behavior.

If Swindoll is correct, and I think he is, then what is the new perspective that we must learn? It is simply that we live in a fallen world, and because of it, pain and suffering will not depart during life on earth no matter how spiritual we are. Bad things *will* happen to Christians as well as to unbelievers.

Pastor Bob unwittingly reinforced a false belief with his advice. Ann, Pete, feuding spouses, and the parents of the teens with serious problems were expecting to find a series of "biblical" behaviors to make their world work according to their desires and expectations, eventually providing happiness and joy. They had questions and wanted answers. They had problems and wanted solutions. Bob responded to their pressure and failed because of a wrong, unbiblical perspective about life in a fallen world. A study of the heroes of Scripture shows they were molded into men and women of God through suffering. If suffering is something that can't be avoided no matter how spiritual we are, then what would God have us do?

Community

The closest thing to Heaven, while living life this side of the grave, should be the fellowship of Christians living in community. Believers should be bearing burdens, sharing joys, and richly enjoying the good things of God with the hope that someday, maybe soon, joy will no longer be mixed with pain and suffering. But for now, a grief shared is half a grief; a joy shared is a greater joy.

A father recently reflected on a seemingly small incident that brought him great joy. His son had recently left home for college, his first time away from home. The father, like many others, wished he had done some things differently in the past in relation to his wife and children. He was beginning to face some harsh realities that fathers should face at some point in their lives—the earlier the better. He saw that other matters had taken higher priority than relationships, and he prayed that his sins of omission wouldn't prevent future communication.

His son faced some hard times at school and wanted to talk with someone. He chose his parents. In spite of past failures, blow-ups, quick and superficial answers to questions, he still called. Communication was open. Community was a reality. The son was willing to share his sorrows as well as his joys. The relationship was intact!

But are our relationships intact in our churches? Do our prayer meetings reflect our real personal struggles? Would we allow our burdens to be shared by others? Would we know how to bear others' burdens? Are these struggles lovingly put into biblical perspective in rich, intimate community? I think not.

Ann and Pete are fictitious people, but their dilemmas are all too common. We completely ignore spiritual commands to bear burdens, weep with those who weep, and listen thoroughly before we speak. We can't fix the Anns and Petes of the world, but we need to prune our shrubs and trim our hedges so our simplistic and superficial solutions don't drive away people like Ann and Pete who are desperately searching to fill a personal vacuum. Solutions like "don't think about it" and "don't be so selfish" fail to communicate anything useful. People hear only "I shouldn't have any longings." But in Scripture God never condemns us for having longings. He simply tells us to face them on His terms.

We can help Ann and Pete face reality on God's terms by combining truth with costly love and acceptance. Ann and

Pete don't know what love and acceptance are. The word *grace* may have a dictionary definition, but to them it is foreign experientially. Our attempts to fix everything usually drive Ann and Pete further from understanding and experiencing grace. Human pain and suffering must be placed in biblical perspective or a vision of a growing church and reaching the lost for Jesus Christ will be a future illusion.

Bob's training was inadequate to face the enormous problems in our world today. He was trained to know the facts of Scripture. His training was primarily didactic, factual presentations of biblical truth. He had factual answers to questions and factual solutions to problems. He kept his distance from the reality of people's lives by providing quick answers and behavioral solutions. Bob didn't know how to be a refuge and model a biblical love to a needy world.

It is rare in post-Christian America for a child to grow up in a solid family where a committed love is modeled, felt, taught, and understood. We are far more than behaving beings; if we are going to live effectively for Christ, we need to have our hearts saturated with a solid understanding of God's love. Christianity is far more than compliance with an acceptable standard of behavior. If there isn't an internal reality, a genuine peace, then either Christianity isn't true or we have somehow missed a major message of Scripture. I believe we have missed the message.

We have "Westernized" Scripture by seeing short-term behavioral change as biblical and by defining and describing sin behaviorally. This enables us to have answers to all questions and solutions to all problems. We need a deeper view of man, sin, and salvation—a deeper view that directly faces the fact that we Christians, individually and corporately, are not really impacting our culture for Jesus Christ.

4

Community

Before the church formalized its essential functions into programs, orders of service, and other rituals, early believers were active in four areas. According to Acts 2:42, they met to learn from the apostles' teaching, to enjoy fellowship, to remember the Lord in worship (the Lord's Supper), and to pray. There must have been a tremendous vitality and reality to these gatherings, as 3,000 souls were added to the local group of believers in one day (verse 41). Somehow for Ann and Pete and many others, the church is not displaying a vitality that is drawing new converts to Christ, Scripture, or community. Somehow that early reality must be recaptured if we are to affect this world for Christ.

Four Basics of Community

Consider first the apostles' teaching. Many in our culture today have abandoned absolutes based on the Judeo-Christian value system. We have turned inward for answers rather than to God. As we do so, the moral corruption that emerges testifies to Romans 1:18-32: pursuit of self is destructive foolishness. When God is removed from our thinking, perversion and violence aren't far behind.

God's absolutes are essential to the Christian who desires to avoid the devastation brought about by accepting the lies of humanism and unbelief in any form, lies that promise something they can't deliver. In the Word of God, the apostles' doctrine, we find the absolutes we desperately need to know God and live with one another in a manner that both pleases God and is clearly in our best interest as well. If what pleases God isn't in our best interest, then He isn't the loving Being He claims to be. Our culture rejects God's absolutes partly because it doubts His love.

The second area, Christian fellowship, is equally vital. In a world where family commitment is becoming nonexistent, we need a stable community of believers committed to God's best for one another. Real community is a vanishing commodity in our society, whether it be a relational network among believers, the nuclear and extended family, or other organizations such as the church. The need for genuine community and intimate fellowship in the church is greater than at any time in our culture. Indeed, community may be God's key means of sustaining the values that keep our faith pure and growing and our species surviving.

Worship, the third aspect of the early church, flows out of an appreciation that God has pulled us out of the stream of humanity headed for destruction and has made us citizens of His Kingdom. Life in a fallen world will not work according to our expectations and demands. But as believers we have been "called out" to face reality: though this life is less than perfect and at times terribly painful, we have a hope unbelievers cannot share.

Tragically, we have perverted the gospel message by making the false assumption that salvation will make life easier. The truth remains that salvation does not in this life deliver us completely from the consequences of the Fall, the fact of pain and suffering. But through His grace, God has equipped us to meet the challenges of a corrupt nature and a fallen world with spiritual resources. He has also promised us that this life of frustration will be only for a season. This hope that only the believer can have, properly understood, produces worship and deep appreciation for the finished work of Jesus Christ. Someday, perhaps soon, we shall be in His presence forever, never again to feel pain or sorrow.

Finally, Christians in the early church met for prayer. When we meet for prayer, it is rare that anyone makes requests other than "safe" ones. The real struggles of Ann and Pete rarely surface for we prize appearance and acceptance more than Christlikeness. Usually, Ann and Pete don't value holiness enough to risk exposure and possible rejection. And the rest of their prayer group doesn't value compassion enough to wade into the mud of their lives. Why should Ann and Pete risk having their souls shredded when the church doesn't demonstrate the kind of Spirit-led sensitivity and care that empowers prayer?

But if Ann's and Pete's issues are not discussed, then community will not develop and the apostles' doctrine will not be seen as relevant to life. A genuine understanding of what God has done cannot develop in a vacuum. Unless the Cross and the Resurrection have something to do with the issues that dominate Ann's and Pete's lives, those great doctrines seem to people like mere words.

Relevant teaching, enabling fellowship, heartfelt worship, and spiritually discerning prayer lead to a Christian community that faces life with appropriate transparency, vulnerability, and mutual ministry. Such community is not an opportunity for a pity party, but a deepening of relationship that enables other-centered ministry.

A Personal Void

A major problem American evangelical churches are facing is that, although many people profess faith in Jesus Christ, few display the strong Christian lifestyle that should result from these professions. In fact, if "lordship salvation" is biblical, perhaps fewer than 20 percent of those sitting in the pews of our evangelical churches are saved. (Lordship salvation basically states that if works don't follow profession of faith, the profession is not saving faith.)

As a former seminary professor, I (Bill) have worked with young men and women who were involved with drugs, immorality, and other clearly sinful behaviors. At the same time, they were pursuing graduate studies in Bible, leading to careers as pastors and missionaries. Is the problem simply that they were never saved? Each one that I talked to clearly knew God's plan of salvation. Many had even led others to the Savior, but privately and sadly admitted, "I offered them eternal life, but the new relationship in Christ for me seems so superficial. I feel like a hypocrite." What's wrong? Were they not truly saved? If they were, should their experience have been different?

I took an informal poll in one of my graduate classes. The results were sobering. The number of students who came from broken homes, alcoholic parents, and other devastating backgrounds was staggering. I doubt if 20 percent came from solid families where Jesus Christ was truly honored. I consider it a tribute to Christian schools that people are coming looking for answers to the tragedies they have seen and experienced all their lives. But an equal tragedy is that much of our Bible education ignores this reality.

Can we deal with these issues by merely presenting the facts of Scripture, in an acquisition-performance model (learn facts, change behavior), or do we need to build in the reality of community: fellowship, prayer at a deep, personal level, and sound biblical teaching as it relates to life in a nearly post-Christian America?

Suffering today in America is shatteringly real! People in our churches come from tragic backgrounds: broken homes, alcoholic parents, sexual abuse. People in the pastorate, on the mission field, and in other Christian ministries also come from these backgrounds. When they say they know how to lead someone to the Lord, but they themselves have not experienced any real change or supernatural healing, what are we to conclude? Were they never saved because there is no "peace" in their soul, no level of apparent appropriate works, and no freedom from besetting sin? If that's true, then what do we, the church, have to offer those people? A salvation that doesn't produce what we expect or a community that doesn't know how to deal with defeat?

Salvation does not abruptly change all of the sinful thoughts, patterns, and values that drive us, or heal all the broken places in our lives. At the cross, our sin was laid on Him and His righteousness was given to us. We were given the Spirit of God to begin a process: to expose our fallen values and our sinful strategies. We were given all we need for progressive and radical change. But we will not feel whole experientially this side of Heaven. There will be struggle, a struggle the unbeliever can't have because he does not have the Spirit of God, the Word of God, and the people of God helping him to face and change the continuing reality of sin in his life and his environment.

When Adam fell, his relationships with God and his wife were severed. He ran from God and sinfully began a futile attempt to make life work on his terms. This foolishness doesn't disappear when we're saved, but the power, moment by moment, to become more aware of this foolishness has been given to us. However, we must exercise our will and take advantage of God's resources. We must actively respond to our new reality and begin to "work out our salvation."

Perform or Perish

What does it mean to "work out our salvation"? What is the process of sanctification? Are we to perform according to a standard in order to prove to ourselves and others that we are really saved? Or are we drawn to the One who has so graciously saved us and brought us into a permanent, intimate relationship with our Creator—a relationship that experience can't sever, that can profoundly change our ways of living, and that quenches the thirst of parched souls? Do sincere appreciation for God's love and deep hunger for His presence draw us toward holiness?

While one might state that being drawn to God is obviously more biblical than performing up to a standard, I submit that performing is the unfortunate reality in North American Christianity. The solution offered to people like Ann and Pete with severely dysfunctional backgrounds is, "Put it out of your mind and try harder." Have you ever tried very hard to put something out of your mind and had it keep coming back with increasing intensity? Denial doesn't work! And where is the Spirit of God involved? It seems moral effort and power of the Spirit are often synonymous in the minds of well-meaning but ineffective spiritual advisors.

When moral effort doesn't work, the next bit of advice is, "Be patient; God will change you." The implication is that if you try hard enough, God will grant His peace. But the problem with this view is that it defines and measures Christian growth behaviorally. If these behaviors don't take place, then we tell the person he doesn't have saving faith. "How, then, do I get saving faith?" he asks. Answer: "By proving it in your behavior." The argument is circular. Where does it leave the suffering Christian? In total despair! If he's truly saved, works should follow. If there is no evidence, salvation is assumed to be nonexistent. Man defines and measures "works" by outward compliance to a code of behavior—not at all what James had in mind when he declared faith would be self-evident.

I have talked to people who are convinced they are not saved and, even though they want to be, are further convinced they aren't of the elect and therefore can't be. They expected

"works" to be natural and easy. They had no concept of faith
They were never taught!

This view of sanctification doesn't produce Christlike
character. At best, it produces superficial compliance. At worst,
it produces rigid, legalistic performance and pride. None of
these options sees man as he really is or effects inward change
at the level of basic understandings, driving values, subliminal
beliefs, or motivations. It is essential that our motive for obedience be neither fear nor pride, but rather the fact that we are
being drawn to Christ out of a deep, heartfelt appreciation for
His gift of salvation. Man should be defined by more than mere
overt behavior. He is a being designed by God to function in an
intimate relationship with God and with fellowman.

Sanctification defined by outward behavior violates the
nature of the gift of salvation, its rich enjoyment, and its motivating power. We are driven to despair if our behavior doesn't
measure up to manmade codes of behavior, which are used by
some "spiritual" leaders as motivators (when in fact such codes
are only manipulators).

When we look at the church today, we see attacks from
both the outside and the inside. Outside, we see the lie of
humanism and other false belief systems and the promise that
life is made meaningful by the gratification of appetites. Paul
speaks of this in his letter to the church at Philippi. Chapter
3, verse 19 tells us that their god is their appetite or belly, an
emptiness that can never be filled, and that self-effort in this
direction guarantees destruction. Man was created by God and,
without God, can never adequately deal with the felt void inside
himself. The enticement of sin to make life meaningful is that it
gives quick relief from pain. The problem is that we need more
and more sin to maintain a level of gratification. When we turn
to sin, we become enslaved to a master that drives us to deeper
and deeper enslavement, perversion, violence, and despair. Sin
works! But only for a season. And its pull is reaching more and

more believers with the love of instant gratification and relief from pain.

Unfortunately, from the inside, the church perverts truth when it communicates that God will take away pain and sorrow and make us happy in this life if we measure up to a "biblical" standard. That is a false expectation. We become addicted and enslaved to teaching a standard of performance that God knew we could never achieve. Growth becomes moral effort rather than deep appreciation for the grace of God to cover our inability to measure up to His standards. Those in positions of influence and authority in the church are unknowingly resorting to a false doctrine in demanding superficial compliance to a "New Testament Law" to "help" us feel secure. But it's having the opposite effect!

Sanctification By Gratitude

Our salvation is free. The gospel is not merely a set of facts to be believed, but a relationship to be entered into by faith (John 17:3, Ephesians 2:8-9). I don't have to do anything but accept the gift. Praise God! I will never measure up to a standard. I don't have to. Christ knew I couldn't; therefore, He made salvation, past and present, totally dependent upon Himself.

Does that set me free to sin? God forbid! Romans 1, Philippians 3:19, and many other Scriptures show me how foolish and destructive sin is. He set me free to pursue holiness without fear that relapse into sin would cause me to lose my relationship with Him. If that isn't motivation to be drawn to Him and to willingly serve Him, we have no concept of who He is or what He has done on our behalf. Understanding this should have a dramatic effect on our lifestyle.

So why aren't more Christians dramatically affected by gratitude for such grace? Too often, the effect is low because they pursue outward holiness only. They don't understand how deeply sin's tendrils have penetrated the core of their souls.

They don't see that their very being is bent in a wrong direction. Therefore, they expect salvation to be a quick escape from a surface struggle. They are shocked when the escape is not quick, and there is often no one to come alongside and encourage them to face ugly truths about themselves and pursue the taxing battle of unlearning deeply ingrained sinful patterns.

When our mind-set is "standardized performance" to assure us of a relationship with God, we are doomed to despair. But when I see in God's Word that my relationship is secure because of the personal sacrifice of Christ, my motivation is gratitude, not fear. Now I have the Spirit of God to draw me to Him, and I am no longer hopelessly shackled by what Christ removed on the cross. I am now free to follow, where before I had neither the choice nor the resources.

What a lesson for us to learn in our relationships with others, to learn to love as God does, not demanding compliance in return, but giving others a safe relationship where they can honestly bring the deepest personal struggles to the surface without fear of rejection! What a foundation for building true community in the church of Jesus Christ! What a powerful motivation to live for Him!

Compassion Versus Obedience

Somehow we have come to see empathy and compassion for sinners as weak or sinful. We fear that compassion gives people an excuse for disobedience. But I believe there is a biblical balance. Jesus entered into the pain of the sinful without becoming a sinner. I must have compassion for those caught up in sin. They are desperately trying to fill a personal vacuum—a tragic impossibility! Women who have been molested hate men so much that they often avoid intimacy of any kind or give their bodies but not their persons to men. They are destroying themselves. Men are looking for "a meaningful one-night stand," as I saw on a bumper sticker. They go deeper and deeper into sin,

looking for what will never be found. They are desperately trying to fill God-given longings to connect as people. Christians
are caught up in these lies in every area of life, not just in sexual
immorality.

No amount of condemnation will convince them that their
direction is destructive. They are terrified to abandon the pleasures of sin, as they provide a temporary respite from personal
pain and agony. And in fact, their longings were built into them
by God and are *never* condemned in Scripture (Isaiah 55:1-2).
The Bible only condemns turning to self and not to God's
authority to deal with the reality of being dependent beings.

So condemnation is not only useless, it is wrong. But the
love of Christ, understood and modeled in Christian community, can provide a place of refuge where reality can be faced
with people who have learned to show compassion. Perfect
love, the love of Christ, is the basis for Christian community. Perfect love is not soft on sin. It gives the sinner a
relationship where he or she can safely face reality and be
wooed to the Savior through the community and involvement
of the saints. At times, the Christian community must be
blunt and confronting. At other times, it must be slow to
speak and deeply compassionate. At all times, it must be
committed to showing grace to the sinner by modeling the
love of Christ.

Risks and Opportunities

What can real community deliver? What can't it deliver? When
we look at the lives of the heroes of Scripture, I am amazed at
how we have perverted the gospel. Paul was imprisoned and
beheaded. Peter was crucified. Stephen was stoned. And our
ultimate example, Jesus Christ, was the crucified Man of Sorrows who was acquainted with grief. But so many come to my
office thinking that the fact that they are saved and attempting
to perform should make life easy. Nowhere is this promised in

Scripture. How can we promise material, physical, and emotional prosperity with the examples of Christ and Paul, Peter, Stephen, and other godly men and women in and out of the Scriptures, saints whose faithfulness resulted in what the world would see as wasted, painful lives? (See Romans 8:31-39.)

Biblical community will not produce utopia. That is impossible this side of Heaven. But God can use community to make His truth relevant to life.

Several years ago, a pastor complained to me (Bill) that the problems in his church seemed overwhelming. He compared his church to several others in his area where the pastors did not seem to have the number or severity of problems that he was facing. But further discussion revealed that his pastor friends had far more formal churches. Their approach to ministry was almost entirely lecture-oriented, and therefore safe! The problem with that philosophy of ministry is that personal faith and growth in Christ cannot be mass-produced through lectures. If it could, we could show videos of great preachers and have growing Christians and churches. In short, what seemed to be smoothly running churches were really institutions that had removed problems by removing the human element.

The pastor with problems in his church was far more in touch with his people through home study/fellowship groups led by elders. At elders' meetings, he was able to discuss vital issues of people's lives, the kinds of issues that should take precedence over buildings and budgets. But he had discovered that when we build community and problems surface, we are also opening the door to confusion. Once Ann opens up about her sexual abuse, pretty soon ten more women confess the same experience, and Pete feels uncomfortable relating to them. To avoid such tension, it is easier to mask reality by institutionalizing and delegating responsibilities to professionals. But when this happens, the power of the gospel takes second place to psychologically trained men and women.

Several years ago, I saw a letter advertising a "refuge" for weary pastors. It said the camp was equipped with trained counselors and other professionals to help them cope with life. This is tragic! Even those trained in Scripture must turn to "experts" who really know about life. If this is true, then Scripture has no practical relevance.

A church that emphasizes community opens the door to problems. Community is no panacea; it will not fix problems, and it makes them harder to gloss over. So when those problems do surface, how do we cope with them?

Several pastors have told me that they will see a member for counseling only one to three times. This superficial involvement is no different from the cold, formal church. My recommendation to pastors with this philosophy is to see only one to three people as long as it take to really help them. The pastor will feel helpless at times, since the process of his counselee's growth is out of his control, but perhaps that is what drives us to prayer and active dependence on God. The pastor will also be unable to counsel the other forty people who want to see him just as badly. He will have to entrust those people to community within his church. He will have to educate his people not to see counseling with the pastor as the solution to their problems.

Change is far more than an act of the will. It requires the people of God, the Word of God, and the Spirit of God confronting, encouraging, sometimes carrying, and always being patient (1 Thessalonians 5:14). We certainly need expository preaching, but we need a way for facts to translate into life. That is a painful process, for we are deeply committed to personal comfort, while God is committed to making us like Christ. The two rarely coexist! And because the process of character development is so painful, few of us allow it to take place to any great degree if we are left to ourselves. God's design is for it to take place in community as reality is faced, problems are aired, biblical perspective is sought, and prayer is continual.

How does this process start? When a leader decides to take a risk. Several years ago, a pastor in one of my classes stated that pastors need a network of fellow pastors with whom to discuss their problems since it was inappropriate to discuss their personal issues in their churches. I responded that with this philosophy of ministry, the pastor was modeling a false state of spirituality. He gave his congregation the impression that he had arrived. As a result, he was unapproachable and his church was cold, formal, and irrelevant to life.

I recently heard several men in their seventies speak about their changing view of God. These men had every struggle that I have. They described their lives as a slowly evolving change in perspective about what is important. They insisted that eternal values do not just happen. Eternal values develop, as Romans 5:3-5 states: through trials that slowly and painfully make us actively depend on the person and work of Jesus Christ, and actively feel the ultimate hope we have in Him.

These men also emphasized their own sinfulness and said they could safely face it because of their security in Christ. To them, God was not a genie in a bottle to invoke when discomfort came, but a God who became real through life's struggles.

Community is perhaps the best way to get men and women who are advanced in the process together with younger men and women who are just beginning. Together, they can bear burdens, weep with those whose process is difficult, and rejoice with those who are rejoicing. Problems may abound. Someone may feel rejected by something wrongly said or done. But our Lord Himself commands us to "love each other" (John 15:17). To follow that command involves vulnerability, and vulnerability is not without risk. Leaders must be trained to minimize risk, but risk cannot be eliminated.

Other problems with a community approach to ministry abound. For example, when does a group leader or pastor bring in the help of someone with more training? How publicly do we discuss deep personal issues, such as past or present sexual sin? What degree of vulnerability is appropriate? A textbook cannot be written with clear, definitive answers to these questions.

However, the alternative—to mask reality and not allow the church under God's authority to deal with the real issues of people's lives—is not a legitimate alternative. It is far better to acknowledge a problem and not know how to handle it than to fear to face it and keep it underground. If the real problems in people's lives are not faced under Scripture's authority, then the opinion of the masses about the Bible's relevance to life will decline even more than it already has.

Biblical community cannot deliver a utopia in the midst of a sinful world. What it can offer to the wounded of the world is a refuge where they can taste a love and community previously unknown. When Christianity provides a sanctuary to those discarded, used, and abused by the world, we then become a place of refuge, personal growth, and witness to the world of the power of Jesus Christ.

5

The Church in Ruins?

A pastor and I (Jeff) were discussing missions. I was describing a meeting in Central America in which thirty-four Mexicans and Costa Ricans met to assess their opportunities against their resources for reaching Central America, the Caribbean, and Cuba.

Central America is tough, but promising. Spiritually hungry people are living in the most precarious political and social circumstances imaginable. When I told my North American pastor guest that we are spending a fortune and wearing out North Americans because we are trying to reach Central America with our traditional approach to sending missionaries, he became visibly uncomfortable. But those thirty-four people were assessing their home turf, and they decided that their professions as lay people were the key to gaining entrance and planting new ministries in those countries.

Much of their discussion dealt with how to design local church settings for their planted ministries that would be in sync with the culture. Their solutions were obviously out of sync with traditional church planting forms. When I said this, my guest exploded, "Why even discuss church? Calvin has told us everything we need to know about church structure!"

Now, I like a lot of what Calvin wrote. Much of what he had to say, along with other great Reformers, is true and needed today. But I also know that Calvin lived in different times. So I asked, "What is systematic theology?" We eventually got around to agreeing very loosely that it is a system of organizing the truths of Scripture.

"Who designs systematic theologies?" I asked next.

"Why, man does," was the reply.

"Is man perfect?" I queried.

"Of course not," was the instant rejoinder.

"Then tell me, where are the weaknesses in Calvin's treatment of the church?"

My friend blustered, "There are none!"

As you can imagine, that ended our conversation.

We need to find our roots for ministry in Scripture, not manmade systems. Some of the rubble the church has become is simply remains of strategies, practices, methods, systems, and traditions that originated in the world, not the Word. Where are the Calvins, Luthers, and Zwinglis of our day who will take a fresh look at what is needed?

We have to face the painful, embarrassing fact that the church is in ruins. Our vitality is gone. Instead of numbers of new believers filling our churches in Acts 2:47 fashion, we have numbers of transfers moving from one church to the next. In stating church goals, a recent denominational publication listed a striking set of action verbs: to explain, to preach, to teach (four times), to guide, to motivate, to lead, and to build (buildings). Laudable as these goals are, where are we to learn, to serve, to reach, to sacrifice, to build (lives), to honor (God), and to reproduce? Where are the Nehemiahs who will look at the rubble as foundations for the future? Where are the Ezekiels who will stand in the gap while growth is rekindled? Where are the Isaiahs who will say, "Here am I, send me"? Our foundations for the future lie in the people of God, the Word of God, and the Spirit of God.

We've looked at our culture, at where the church is in relation to that culture, and at some essential features the church is lacking if we are to reach the culture. We've stacked a glimpse of biblical community up against the way most of us do things now, and we've noticed some gaps. In the remainder of this book, we'll explore some alternatives to business as usual. We'll offer perspectives rather than easy answers, for there are no easy answers in a world where God wants us to learn to be totally, terrifyingly dependent upon Him. The first concept we'll examine is the difference between a movement and an institution.

PART TWO

A BIBLICAL
ALTERNATIVE

6

A New Beginning

S uppose you are the central figure in a potentially multinational movement. Potential because it hasn't happened yet. But your ideas, your company, are at the vanguard of something new and extraordinary. Word has spread like wildfire. Some traditionalists in the industry, obviously threatened, resist your ideas, speaking out against them.

For the most part, however, the marketplace is flocking to your door. There is an almost desperate need for your services. Already you envision growth taking you around the world.

And then you discover you have terminal cancer. Two months to live.

So, you call in your team. It's time to do some strategic planning. How can you keep this interest in your services alive? What can be done to ensure that the embryonic movement you have founded doesn't collapse? There is so much to consider: marketing, funding, communication, management demands, leadership, and so on. What is really important? Crucial? Will those you leave behind be adequate for the challenges they face?

The Survival of a Movement

Part of how you answer the questions depends on how you view movements. Janet Hock, in an excellent research paper entitled *Where the Wind Blows*, identifies some common characteristics of spiritual movements. I quote them here with her permission.

1. "Movements are hard to define." A movement can be simply an ongoing effort to achieve change through activities that are typically spontaneous, nontraditional, and noninstitutional. Attempts to control or direct a movement tend to kill the initiating or inhibiting focus of the movement.

2. "Movements are prompted by the Holy Spirit, who convicts future leaders of their individual sin." For our purposes, a spiritual movement can be controlled or directed only by the Spirit of God. The key players in the movement are called, developed, and placed by God, not man.

3. "In prompting movement, the Holy Spirit uses not only a particular need, concern or expectation, but the perception that the necessary resources are available to cause that change." Here is where human instrumentality, in the providence of God, enters in. It is the nature of God to insist on change and the nature of man to resist it. But all the while, God is committed to working through people. These needs, concerns, and expectations are people-centered.

4. "Movements change as they go through different stages of development in which different types of leaders emerge." Restlessness produces reformers who are later replaced by strategists. In the final stages, administrators produce an institution that is accepted by society but is less enthusiastic for its original concerns.

5. "Movements are products of their particular time and culture." Without some relationship to society at large, a movement cannot be sustained. It draws life from a need to change centered in people.

6. "Although most movements initiate renewal, eventually

they themselves need reform." This follows from our tendency to control and direct movements—to quantify, measure, and formulate—which turns them into institutions.

7. "Movements emphasize social action." A social conscience, in this case Spirit-led, inhabits movements.

8. "Movements originate at a grass-roots or populist level attracting a diverse membership."

9. "Movements are often hindered by traditional methods of social progress." Since movements generally incorporate unconventional forms of change, standard methods and assumptions may be irrelevant.

In our case, if the movement founded by the person with terminal cancer is spiritual, then he needs to consider the implications of these characteristics. To attempt to orchestrate a movement guarantees its demise by definition. Movements must be in touch with the realities of their times, not some previous generation's. Institutions are not movements, but movements can become institutions. To disengage from the social problems of the day is a step away from movement and the Spirit's leading. To define too clearly is to divide—movements must be trans-denominational. For survival, movements require willingness to examine needs with an open mind, as free as possible from bias.

Looking for Formulas, Missing God

Suddenly, the list our fictitious CEO developed looks irrelevant. Survival of the movement does not depend on strategic planning, marketing formulas, or time management. The church faces the same questions as it seeks to keep the movement of the gospel alive in its generation—the lost being saved, the saved being edified. My (Jeff's) friend Rusty Stephens captures this dilemma in his parable of the fishermen.

Once there was a team of fishermen. They fished for a living. Founded and banded together by a zealous, creative, master fisherman named Joseph Flounder, affectionately referred to by friends as "Joe," over the years they had developed an excellent array of fishing tackle, equipment, and skills that allowed them to be very productive at catching fish.

They were a band of brothers who really loved each other and loved fishing. They recruited many new candidates, mostly by pointing out how noble fishing was and that people ought to be engaged in that activity. The number of skilled fishermen multiplied and influenced the entire fishing industry. Joe used to say, "Give a man a fish, and he'll have food for a day. But teach him how to fish, and he'll have food for the rest of his life." Joe also said, "Anyone can catch fish, especially with a little help from his friends!"

At first, the founder developed groups of fishermen candidates, banded them together, and fired them with the vision for catching thousands of fish. He fished with them. He often said, "God gave you a lot of leading when He gave you a brain!" and, "Fishing is simply going to where the fish are and catching them. By all means, catch some!"

The teams would wrestle together concerning how to accomplish the vision of catching thousands of fish. They developed varying methods, depending on their preferences and where they were fishing. Some stood in the surf with rods and reels, casting out into the ocean. Others built boats in which to get to schools of fish offshore. Some even built a boat with a screen door in the bottom so they could see the fish better. But they drowned the first time they got underway.

Eventually, the founder died, but the work was well established. In fact, it had become an organization. Thousands of fishermen were catching millions of fish. And hundreds more were being recruited. There was a fish in every pot.

Over a period of time, the recruiting and developing of new fishermen tended to shift from passing on basic principles and values related to successful fishing to "how-to's."

The fishermen trainers (a role that had developed) could get new fishermen deployed quicker with those methods. Eventually, boats were prohibited, because the influential ones cried, "That's not our thing." It was too time-consuming and complicated to build boats, and plenty of fish were available in the surf.

A given fisherman would fish a spot for a while, but once he'd recruited and trained a replacement, he'd move to another place and start over. Eventually, it became standard that you fished in one place for four weeks, then turned it over to your replacement and moved.

Even so, there got to be too many fishermen, and they were crowding one another. So group tactics were developed. At the command of the overfisherman (another new role), they would cast in unison out into the surf. That way, no matter what the wind, their lines would not get tangled. After a while, they began to realize that fish, once hooked, didn't swim to shore in a straight line, so they developed the practice of cutting the line on any fish that didn't swim straight, in unison with the others. They lost a lot of fish, but they still caught a lot, too.

They began to keep records of how many fish were caught per day, and who caught each one. This took a lot of time and energy, but most of the fishermen thought it was worth it. And it made them feel really good to get personal credit for the fish they were catching. Sometimes there were arguments over whose fish was whose, since one would bait the line, another would cast it, and several would help land the fish, particularly the large ones.

Over the years, several fundamental things began to change. Due to the greenhouse effect in that part of the world, the inshore water warmed up. Also, the Gulf Culture Stream shifted further offshore. This caused increasing numbers of fish to school farther from the shoreline. Eventually 50 percent of the uncaught fish were farther out than the surf fishermen could cast.

Also, hooking a fish receded in importance. Originally considered the essential starting point of the process, it became only a desired portion of the fishing process. More and more fishermen teams were developed that primarily transferred already-hooked fish to their lines and skillfully reeled· them toward shore. As the fish moved farther offshore, it took longer to reel them in. So many fishermen would reel in awhile, then get impatient and quit reeling, exclaiming, "That fish didn't meet the standards." Often those fish would be swimming in as fast as they could. They were just farther out. But this made no difference to the fishermen. They would pass off those fish. And it seemed that someone else was always there to pick up those fish and play with them for a while.

Eventually, the numbers of fish being caught decreased noticeably. Some fishermen pointed this out, but most of the others considered this an irritation. They blamed the fish, and often retorted "The Lord Fisher hasn't called us to be success- ful, just faithful!"

Some fishermen questioned the practice of moving every four weeks, especially if a fisherman hadn't figured out how to catch fish at his current location.

Some fishermen recommended doing whatever it took to find out where the fish were and developing ways to get off- shore into the schools of fish. They were usually silenced with "That's accommodating the fish!" or "We don't have time to figure that out. It might take years!" Some even said, "If we go out there, we might get wet or drown!"

Things got so bad they decided to have a consultation on fishing, so they got together in the mountains. One poor soul was assigned the task of presenting a talk on how to fix every- thing that was wrong with their fishing. They scheduled him for Sunday evening and gave him twenty minutes.

Do you see the problem? The fishermen need a new beginning—one that causes each generation to have ownership of the mission in its own unique way. Our friend with cancer needs to consider this; so does the church.

Life in the Baby Boom

Why a new beginning? Because people and times change. Consider John Q. Boomer. Those who identify with John's experiences are probably of his generation. The church, if it is to participate in movement—the expansion of the Kingdom of God in the hearts and minds of men and women—must adapt its message to John's world. Not the world of his father or the world of his son, but John's world.

John was born into a large family. His parents came from different backgrounds—one of wealth and one of poverty, one of secular roots and one with a religious heritage. Both eventually became highly successful professionals.

Failure was not tolerated in John's family. The children learned to excel, or to blame others, make excuses, and lie. Love was conditional on performance, and expressions of affection or acceptance were nonexistent. The parents eventually separated twice, the final time ending in divorce. John's father was an alcoholic who physically abused his wife and sons and sexually abused his daughter. He died of complications related to alcoholism at age forty-five. The daughter was institutionalized briefly, then underwent psychiatric treatment for two years. One son briefly pursued criminal interests while another got into drugs. John found escape in athletics, academics, and appetites. The daughter still is not mentally competent in some areas today. The oldest son still breaks the law, though he has learned how not to get caught. John and the youngest son have straightened out for different reasons and are successful professionals in their own right.

By the time John was in the military, he was a cold, hard,

unfeeling, very driven man. Vietnam did not help; there success was measured in body counts. It was safe not to have friends you might have to stuff in a body bag tomorrow. John came home convinced of man's depravity, and what's more—his own. Then John got married.

For the first few years, things went relatively well. In fact, John became a believer. He and his wife, already a believer, began to grow in the Lord. But because of dysfunctional elements in both their histories, things began to break down. There followed four very dark years. John became depressed and fought burnout. His wife lived in a world of her own. It was more a matter of providence than desire that they remained faithful to each other.

The years went by, and children came and grew. John fished one two-year-old son off the bottom of a lake. Another son nearly drowned in a pool and a daughter took a plunge off a second-story porch. One of the sons suffered from an undiagnosed kidney ailment reminiscent of the kidney failure experienced by John's sister. John's mother died unexpectantly from a particularly gruesome cancer, and the doctors thought for a while that John's wife might have malignant tumors. A daughter began to struggle with depression and through some bizarre behavior influenced the school to have her parents reported for child abuse even though they were quite innocent.

Still quite successful, having weathered the tough early years of marriage, and essentially a good parent, John's character deficiencies caught up with him. Coworkers approached him with humiliating evidence of his need. The choice was to quit his profession or voluntarily remain and learn the discipline of humility. Several years of counseling and growth followed.

Lest you feel sorry for John, remember that he has had many good experiences in life as well. He actually has become a secure, sensitive, and caring individual. John is not a perfect person, mind you, but he is healthy.

For John Q. Boomer's generation, these kinds of experiences are not unusual. They affect his world view and receptivity to the gospel. Methods, formulas, programs, and messages designed to create and capitalize on redemptive opportunities in his father's generation will totally miss John. This means that John and others like him are not within the cultural reach of most existing local churches.

John is coming from a new and growing perspective in our culture. Not only does he come from a very dysfunctional family, but also his concept of God, if he has one, is extremely distorted. He thinks that if there is a God, how could He allow all the devastations John and others in his generation have gone through?

The Quick Fix

A major characteristic of this generation is a desire for a quick fix for their situations. John wants results. Ann and Pete also want results. Life has not worked according to their hopes and desires. Now that their lives are linked to the Sovereign God of the universe, they have expectations and hopes. They want to know what to do now that they are Christians so that they can partake of God's promises and blessings.

This desire to put God into a box and find a divinely ordained formula for success isn't new. In Exodus 19:4-5, the Lord said to Moses, "This is what you are to say to the house of Jacob and what you are to tell the people of Israel: 'You yourselves have seen what I did to Egypt, and how I carried you on eagle's wings and brought you to myself. Now if you obey me fully and keep my covenant, then out of all nations you will be my treasured possession.'"

After hearing these words, all Israel said was just tell us what to do and we'll do it (verse 8). What the Israelites,

John, Pete, and Ann failed to realize is that God's standard is perfection, pure actions flowing out of a pure heart. For fallen, depraved man, His standard is impossible. Then why did He give us such an impossible task? So that we would be driven to Him and His grace, not to a set of behaviors to measure up to and thereby reap temporal benefits.

Israel wanted a set of rules to follow, a formula that would ensure control over her destiny. John Q. Boomer, Pete, and Ann also want to control their destinies by performing appropriate biblical tasks. Even Pastor Bob wants control. He wants to provide biblical solutions for his struggling church members—solutions that he can understand, prescribe, and see predictable results from, so that his church will run smoothly and successfully. But all of these attempts, no matter how noble they seem, are efforts to manipulate God and our environment to make things happen according to our plans and under our control. They are a search for a nonexistent spiritual formula that leaves out the power of God.

As I read Scripture, I find that God gives us much latitude in figuring out how to apply His truth to specific situations. He does not give husbands a step-by-step approach as to how to love their wives. He simply describes how Christ loved the church and put her above his personal comfort. A husband must look at his wife's background, blind spots, gifts, and so on to see how best to model Christ's love to her. There is no universal formula or specific steps. A husband has to study the ideal of how Christ loves His bride and prayerfully decide how to apply it in his specific case. He is dependent upon the Spirit of God and the people of God to help him apply what he reads in the Word of God.

A formula shifts the emphasis from "What should I do to allow the Spirit of God to work through me more effectively?" to "What should I do to produce the result I want?" The latter relies on human behavior to bring about change, and often lets human desires color the goals of change. The former trusts the Spirit of the living God to bring change and allows Him to set the agenda.

The leader of the fictional movement with which this chapter opened was faced with the problem of sustaining his movement. He began to quantify, explain, define, and organize in order to perpetuate what God seemed to have begun. He was focusing on behaviors designed to produce a product. But even though we begin to do all of these things for all of the right reasons, a movement can shift to an institution, and following the Spirit can shift to having Him bless our efforts. When this happens, leaders (pastors) become isolated in their growing institution and out of touch with the people. What God has begun is destroyed.

When I (Bill) discuss with pastors the severity of the cases I see daily, the two typical reactions are "I had no idea things were that bad" (which indicates isolation from the problem) and "I'm glad we have people like you trained to deal with those cases" (which indicates, tragically, that theological training is inadequate for real-life situations).

How can we develop churches that will relate to single parents (mostly women, since men seem to be abdicating responsibility), married couples who have never seen a biblical family modeled to them, bulimics, former drug and alcohol abusers, and the many other kinds of dysfunctional people who are longing to put their lives together? They want formulas and fixes. We attempt to provide those fixes, but as with Ann and Pete and their pastor, fixes don't work and the lines of communication are breaking down. How can we rejuvenate a movement that began 2,000 years ago when we can't find a universal formula that seems to get results?

The Lord Jesus was in a similar predicament to that of our CEO with cancer. Burdened with founding a movement, He would depart before it got off the ground. His followers certainly did not understand that His death was not the end. What new beginning would Jesus encourage His team to commit themselves to? Are there instructions for the church in the words Christ left to His disciples just before the cross? If you were Jesus and had one last opportunity to address your disciples, what would you say?

7

The Mind of Jesus

Formulas and People

I (Jeff) know what a formula approach to ministry feels like. Not long ago, an acquaintance began to evangelize me. He used what is often described as lifestyle or friendship evangelism. As our relationship grew over the months, my admiration for his evangelism grew. Everything I teach in evangelism, this fellow modeled perfectly. Other than being a member of a cult, I could find no fault with his approach. Yet instead of recruiting me, it alienated me.

Let's call my friend Mark. We met in the context of a weekly recreational activity. Mark showed interest in me as a person and admired my profession. At his initiative, our conversations were often turned away from him and onto me or issues of mutual interest. I was invited to his home several times, and Mark appeared to have an idyllic family, something enviable these days. Mark's ability to weave spiritual content into many of our conversations without giving offense was smooth and natural.

As we jogged together on occasion, Mark would probe for areas in my life, personal and professional, that I was dissatisfied with. The help he offered was always timely, sensitive. He was quick to respond to any opportunity to bring a spiritual dimension into things. Leading questions, invitations to well-thought-through activities, and an obvious effort to spend time with me were all part of a well-planned strategy to create opportunities for dialogue. And that was part of the problem.

Even recognizing Mark's sincerity, I could not escape feeling some resentment that I was part of an agenda, a statistic in a program. In spite of his winsomeness, it was offensively clear that I was an objective, not a person, and that the relationship he was building had ulterior motives. It was easy to reject his beliefs. Sound familiar?

As it became clear that I was not going to prove to be fertile ground, Mark struggled with how to withdraw from the relationship. Everyone has a limited capacity for maintaining relationships, and I'm sure Mark wanted to make room in his life for a more promising prospect. But having worked so hard at pushing our acquaintance into relationship, he realized that to withdraw would send the wrong signals to me, perhaps eliminating any possible future opportunity. His formula failed; even worse, it put Mark in a cul-de-sac with no way out. I must say, his discomfort with this dilemma was enjoyably obvious.

Jesus didn't say, "Build relationships with people to draw them to Me." He said, "Love people." The Holy Spirit naturally moves acquaintances into relationship. We respond to His leading, not to a program or formula. Now, no one denies that tools and methods are important, useful, and needed. But it was clear to me that to Mark the formula had become an end in itself, not a means. He seemed duty-bound to win me over, and focused so totally on getting it "right"—accomplishing the objective—that the "person" got lost in it all. He was totally unaware of how much I felt like a product.

Evangelism is a process, not an event. It's about people, not products or achievement.

Saying and Doing

Recently, a large evangelical organization made the following statement about evangelism. I like it because it seems to balance methods with audience realities and keeps the focus on evangelism as a process: "When Jesus was approached by Nicodemus, He was careful to respond in such a way that Nicodemus was drawn into the conversation. The truth of who Jesus is and the response made possible for all mankind was communicated in a very different way to the Samaritan woman. Understanding your audience in this way (receiver orientation) is crucial to evangelism. Like Jesus, we confront social barriers to communicating the gospel."

Mark drew me into conversation all right, but it was clear he did not accept me as Jesus did Nicodemus and the woman. Mark was more interested in his own need to be involved in ministry than in any real need I might have had.

Contextualizing ministry without compromising Scripture or our calling requires that our actions affirm the gospel we verbally communicate. If we're talking about a just and loving God, we have to treat people with justice and love. That's a tall order. To "do and say" a message requires that we intimately understand the truth we are communicating. The gospel is more than facts about a man who died and somehow lived again. We have to demonstrate as well as describe the reality of a personal relationship with a living Savior, so that the essence of the message is abundantly clear.

That means we can't be content to coast spiritually. If our lives are part of the message, we have to be actively giving the Holy Spirit access to areas we might prefer to keep to ourselves. Here lies the reason many of us would rather tell the gospel than demonstrate it: demonstrating means letting God do whatever it takes to make us just, loving people, and letting people watch the whole messy process. Strictly verbal witnessing, as scary as it can be, is a piece of cake compared to that!

The organization's statement goes on: "Man's condition and God's solution are tough realities to get across to those skeptical, suspicious and even antagonistic toward the gospel. Certain skills and basic tools help in communicating the true meaning of salvation and how one becomes a child of God, a citizen of Christ's Kingdom, and a member of His family. But all this is meaningless if the Holy Spirit does not draw men and women to Christ—convicting them of need, revealing truth, removing the intellectual and emotional obstacles.

"Our evangelism method, therefore, begins and ends with prayer. We encourage our staff to understand the nature of their audience and the essence of the gospel, and to wed the two in relevant communication. A life-style that gives integrity to the message, and a few simple skills and tools to aid in making the message of God's love appropriately clear—these support evangelism efforts. With this approach, the gospel can be shared in a variety of ways, from different portions of Scripture, to many different people and groups."

This is a far cry from the depersonalizing approach Mark took in making me his target and our relationship the objective. It is also a small picture of the church in its ministry. Jesus acknowledged and affirmed people, not programs.

Studying an Audience
A newsletter I received not long ago from a friend working for Church Discipleship Ministries describes a church in Southern California that took a non-formula approach to ministry. The pastor took the time to identify his audience: the self-assured, successful, sports-minded, casual, well-educated, over-extended career person who basically has no interest in organized religion. The pastor didn't target these people; he simply identified what was already there.

Pastor Ralph, we will call him, treated his ministry like a mission field and set out to learn the culture. Ralph found ways to meet social and spiritual needs, ways that reveal God's relevance to people's lives. Instead of services and programs designed to make believers feel comfortable in church, Ralph intentionally shifted toward unbelievers. This also required changing terminology (not theology) into the vernacular of the day and place. Today his church has more than 4,000 attending, 70 percent of whom became Christians through the contextualized approach to ministry.

Quite an accomplishment for a young man right out of seminary. Pastor Ralph had to discard most of what he had been taught about formulas for success and trust the Holy Spirit in developing a Christ-centered, lay-led, audience-focused ministry that is tilted toward the unchurched and unreached in society. The result is a movement-minded church rather than a collection of complacent individuals. We will learn more about movement in chapter 8.

While we cannot let results be our criterion for success, we cannot help but rejoice when God blesses our efforts. We must be driven to Scripture to determine our methods, not settle for what works or what seems to work.

Servant Thinking

Jesus was movement-minded; what were His priorities? In spending His last earthly hours with the future leaders of His movement, Jesus outlined the core truths He wanted them to remember. (Some say these men could have been in their late teens to early twenties).

After washing their feet, He asked them, "Do you understand what I have done for you?" (John 13:12; see verses 13-20). A teacher does not wash feet; others serve him. Washing their feet was a departure from the accepted way of doing things. Jesus modeled the servant leadership that movement requires.

There is no benefit in being unconventional just to gain

attention. But some situations do require us to recognize that conventional forms may no longer be serving the functions for which they were designed and, in fact, are now obstacles to overcome. As long as the teacher was viewed as someone to be served, and not the servant, movement would not get off the ground.

Loving others in this way, in the way Jesus loved them in so many things, was new to the disciples. Jesus said so Himself (John 13:31-35). Giving your life for others may not seem so astounding to us, but to men accustomed to living under the Law, a lifestyle based on relationship took time to percolate!

In Luke 10:25-29, we find another enigmatic relational idea. Prior to this, the Seventy have been sent out. Upon their return, they gather with Jesus to recount their exploits. You can imagine them sitting around responding to each other and Jesus. Perhaps seated on the ground around Jesus, they are animated in their storytelling and respond to Jesus' questions with ready excitement.

But there is a ringer in the crowd. A lawyer suddenly stands up to test Jesus, probably to trip Him up in front of this group and so discredit Him. He asks about eternal life. Knowing that the Law proscribed for a Jew his relationship to God, Jesus asks the lawyer what the Law says. The lawyer answers his own question by summing up the Pentateuch in terms of *relationships*: loving God and others as we love ourself. The amazing thing is that Jesus confirms this one-statement summary as being correct!

The point is that movement moves forward on relationships. It is a function of networks, not of organizational effort. We too easily get wrapped up in organizational issues rather than personal relationships. *Any organizational effort should be geared to facilitate loving God and others in a deepening relational community.* Instead, organization often inhibits this core function. What is important to Jesus in this statement is God's expectation for right relationships, not right programs—which the lawyer would have made out of the ceremonial law.

The importance of this fact cannot be overemphasized. If the two greatest commandments have to do with relationships, and if we want to rebuild a ruined church, then we should pour our greatest efforts into nurturing relationships between believer and believer, and between believer and God.

The lawyer finds himself trapped, just as he had hoped to trap Jesus. Wishing to justify himself, he raises the question of who his neighbor is. Certainly, to this Jew, "neighbor" does not include Gentiles or Samaritans. Jesus capitalizes on this prejudice and uses the story of the good Samaritan to drive His point home. The Seventy, sitting and listening, don't realize what a valuable lesson they are witnessing. Relationships are one of the few things that can carry the content of movement unimpaired across social and cultural barriers.

Freedom from Anxiety

With all the change the disciples were facing, it is easy to understand their anxiety. In His farewell address, Jesus commanded them, "Do not let your hearts be troubled" (John 14:1). He knew change brings difficult adjustments; there is a real need to offer hope (14:2-3). Thomas and Philip expressed this need in their questions (14:5,8). In response, Jesus promised the Holy Spirit (14:16-18,26-27) who would come alongside as a helper and teacher, bringing recollection. The result would be peace—not a peace the world knows, based on outer circumstances, but peace only Jesus can give based on inward realities. The key to experiencing this peace in the midst of change—the key to not being troubled—is the Holy Spirit.

The Holy Spirit is the key to transformation in individuals as well as institutions. In Romans, Paul talks about not being conformed to this world but transformed by the renewal of our minds (12:2). *Metamorphosis* is the word used. It is the same word used to describe the Transfiguration in Matthew 17:2, as well as the change process Paul pictures in 2 Corinthians 3:18. The sense of the word in Romans 12:2 is that something must happen that we are powerless to accomplish ourselves. We find the same idea of making something new in Titus 3:5, where Paul describes the renewing role of the Holy Spirit.

Although we cannot generate metamorphosis through our own effort, we can be obstacles to the change process. In 2 Corinthians 3:18, Paul talks about being unveiled in front of the mirror. Unveiling implies uncovering the roots, revealing what is truly there. This willingness to embrace the truth about who we really are—not to deny, repress, or run from what is there—is the limiting factor in the transformation process. "But we having been unveiled and so are changing" is one way of putting it. Our capacity to change is tied to our ability to face the truth.

Prepare for Pruning
Jesus then turns the topic to how the disciples can get along while He is gone (John 15:1-27). Maintaining a right relationship to Him (15:1-11), to each other (15:12-17), and to the world (15:18-27) is going to require change. And change—transformation—is going to require pruning (15:2). It all begins with abiding in Him; otherwise every effort of ours will amount to nothing (15:5). For movement to bear fruit (15:8), these right relationships must exist.

Jesus closes this thought in verse 17: "This is my command: Love each other." Love from God's perspective, commit to one another, build your relationships and your communities to weather the coming storm of hatred and persecution.

What a radical departure from the perspective of these Jewish believers! They were used to expecting temporal blessing and prosperity in exchange for obedience. But instead of peace and prosperity, obedience will produce that which you naturally do not like. You will be hated because the world hated the Son of God first. Verse 25 says, "They hated me without reason." Jesus is saying, "You will be hated for faithfully proclaiming My message to the world. Expect it!"

With this perspective, we are faced with a disturbing situation. The issue is how we respond to the reality Christ pictured, not "what works." Most programs are designed to promote growth, great movements, prominence, and visible results. We look at huge churches, multiple staffs, great buildings, and perceive it as God's blessing. We certainly cannot deny this possibility, but the words of Christ to the Pharisees in Luke 16:15 might have a modern-day application: "You are the ones who justify yourselves in the eyes of men, but God knows your hearts. What is highly valued among men is detestable in God's sight."

God calls us individually to Christlike character in a community committed to deep relationship and evangelical outreach. Growth is His choice. If programs and formulas were able to generate growth, then we would depend on them and move toward self-sufficiency rather than active dependence—faith—on the sovereignty of God.

An earlier example in John 6 planted the seed for this teaching on suffering. Jesus' followers did not welcome His words in John 6:53-58 concerning eating His flesh and drinking His blood. Their response (6:60), "This is a hard teaching. Who can accept it?" was not a question of difficulty of understanding. It was a question of the difficulty of following Him in His suffering. Peter's response, "Lord, to whom shall we go? You have the words of eternal life" (6:68), faced this harsh reality. Christ's way was the only way even if it meant a lifestyle of self-denial and faith.

Feeling Out of Control
John 16:1-5 continues the same thought. The Lord does not want His people to become confused and go astray when

circumstances, including death, come crashing down on them. Life will seem to be out of control.

Control is the singular issue that surfaces in every problem of life. Husbands want control of their wives (want them to respond in appropriate ways). Wives want a way to change (control) their husbands so they will be more loving and communicative. Parents and children, supervisors and subordinates, pastors and congregations—we all want control.

Even the Apostle Paul initially asked for control in 2 Corinthians 12:7-10. He had a thorn in the flesh that he perceived was getting in the way of ministry, but God would not remove it. In fact, God saw it as helpful. Paul came to the conclusion that it kept him dependent on God, which was the real strength of his ministry. When control slipped away, he was stripped of thinking that he had any real strength in himself.

If you were living at the time of Paul, it would have appeared that his ministry was losing its impact. But looking back from the twentieth century, we see that his loss of control, including imprisonment, left him with only a pen to write letters, letters that God has used to keep His movement going.

After warning His followers of what to expect when they placed themselves in His service, the Lord shifts to the work of the Spirit after His departure (John 16:5-6). He begins by explaining that His departure is really a good thing because it makes possible the coming of the Spirit. The Spirit comes to convict the world of sin and teach the disciples more than Christ had already taught.

Verse 12 has a fascinating perspective. Christ had more to say, but His people were not, at that time, able to bear it. Commentators have suggested several ways that this verse be understood. Some emphasize that we could not fully understand Christ's message without the Spirit's ministry. Another perspective is that what God expects of us as believers is more than could be accomplished without the new work of His Spirit.

Both have validity. Christ had not yet died, and He was asking His disciples to model their lives after His, even to this point of death, to participate in the movement He had initiated. To do that, to see personal death as potentially contributing to their Leader's finished work on Calvary, certainly required the Spirit's help. Certainly dying for enemies was beyond the disciples' capacity. This perspective was and is the utter opposite of natural thinking.

After teaching this radical notion, the Lord softened the facts somewhat by putting physical life into an eternal perspective. Their grief at His departure, the harsh reality of the call to discipleship—all would turn to joy as a mother's anguish turns to joy after the birth of her child.

It's unclear what Jesus is specifically referring to in John 16:22. When will the disciples experience this joy, and how much joy can they expect in this life? Certainly, there was joy when they saw Him again after the Resurrection. But this joy was not free from sorrow. A joy without sorrow will not be reality until He takes us to be with Him. It is the fact of our final joy that allows us to face the trouble that comes in the world. Christ sums up the necessary perspective in verse 33: "I have told you these things, so that in me you may have peace. In this world you will have trouble. But take heart! I have overcome the world."

Facing the Agony

Chapter 17 of John begins with a prayer sequence that is different than many of us have been taught. Jesus prayed for Himself first, then for His disciples, and finally for the larger body of believers. He was deeply troubled by what He faced. A life of faith is not a life of success after success. It is a life of seeing God's perspective—no matter how painful, realizing He has our best interest at heart, and continuing to follow Him. Christ displayed to us what it is like to follow Him by His example of following His Father. He allowed us to see His personal agony in the Garden of Gethsemane. He cried out to His Father three times to come up with another solution. There was none. He asked His disciples to stay awake and pray. They failed. His faith resulted in His crucifixion, but His Father was in total control, raised Him from the dead, and presented Him with His bride.

As He moved into His Father's will, Jesus prayed first for Himself. Although He was concerned with the agony that was ahead, His primary concern was that He would honor His Father in the work He was doing. All the while He was longing for the glory He had with the Father before the world began. He knew His Father could be trusted as He relinquished control to Him. God did not spare His pain, but He honored His faith.

I recently heard a story of a surgeon missionary in a remote area who had to perform surgery on his son without the benefit of up-to-date equipment and anesthesia. His words to his son were, "I may cause you intense pain, but I will never harm you." We need to hear our Father repeating these same words as we enter into Christ's sufferings.

Sin and evil have taken their toll and still do. It was sin and evil that made Christ's death necessary. Until He comes, we cannot escape evil's influence. Christ's prayer for Himself should be our prayer also as we anticipate what He has warned us lies ahead: "Because I know Him, help me complete Your work that others may know You through me as I model Your love to them."

God's Kind of Unity

Jesus then prays for His disciples (17:6-19), who remain in the world after His departure. He prays that they be comforted in their coming trials by the fact that they have a hope the world cannot have. They are no more of the world than He is of the world. His work is finished, but theirs is just beginning.

He concludes by praying for us (17:20-26) as we continue in the movement He began. The theme of His request is that we display to the world an example of intimacy modeled in the Trinity:

" . . . Father, just as you are in me and I am in you. May they also be in us so that the world may believe that you have sent me. I have given them the glory that you gave me, that they may be one as we are one: I in them and you in me. *May they be brought to complete unity to let the world know that you sent me and have loved them even as you have loved me.*" (17:21-23, emphasis mine)

The Lord asks us to model the unity between Him and His Father as the primary message to a lost world of its need of a Savior. In our late twentieth-century churches, we have lost this deep unity and intimate community that characterized the early church. Organizations have replaced community. Programs have replaced relationships. And a clergy class replaces mutual ministry and the opportunity to be a part of a fellowship where one is not only ministered to but has a unique opportunity to minister. (This concept will be discussed further in chapter 12.)

In the examples that opened this book, we do not see the unity Christ spoke of in John 17:21-23. Sam and his pastor may be related well to each other and the Lord, but it is clear the details of Sam's conversion and baptism would be objectionable to the other leaders of the church. So the pastor conceals some things, changing his relationship to the church in subtle, destructive ways. Fred and Jerry, in their disagreement at the elders meeting, certainly are not relating well together. In fact, their hostility toward one another impedes the church's ministry at large. Amanda is searching for right relationship to the Lord, but cannot find someone to help. Her singles pastor is too focused on making his program work. Bill and Ginger view the church as not rightly related to the community they want to reach.

The well-meaning minister using small-group Bible studies as an evangelistic tool (chapter 2) understands the need for right relationships. But his approach to providing them is guaranteed to fail because his institutional methods are irrelevant. The denominational position on evangelism focuses on methods, formulas, programs, events—not on processes or relationships. Programs serve our purposes in that they give us a sense of control. People learning to love in active, other-centered community open the door to modeling the love of Christ.

Total Trust

The issue we must face is the mind of Christ and how He wants us to think. He saw Himself so intimately linked with His Father that He gave total control over to Him. He knew that lack of perceived impact, trials, tribulations, even the Cross, did not indicate final reality. He followed His Father's will, and "When they hurled their insults at him, he did not retaliate; when he suffered, he made no threats. Instead, he entrusted himself to him who judges justly" (1 Peter 2:23). And God allowed Him to die to establish His movement and reconcile His bride, the church.

We have been given the chance to carry on. We must learn to entrust results to the Father and the Spirit. Our responsibility is simply to model Him in the most effective ways possible in the situations where we find ourselves. Culture has changed, but His model still applies. Our challenge is to model Him to a post-Christian culture.

8

The Model

John opens his gospel with a simple assertion: Jesus Christ was with God in the beginning (John 1:2). Now, we can only guess at what Heaven must be like, but certainly it is very different from what we experience on earth. In one sense, it probably has its own culture—its own behavior patterns, norms, values, beliefs, and so on. So when Jesus left His home for ours, He crossed perhaps the greatest cultural boundary there could ever be: that which separates God's Kingdom culture from human culture.

John further refers to the man Jesus as "the Word" (1:1). Jesus is God's self-expression, and He embodies Kingdom values. In another way, the Bible is also God's "Word"; it is also His self-expression and sketches for us the values of the Kingdom. Somehow the Kingdom values Jesus personifies are contained in the Scriptures as well. So these two—the written Word and the Word made flesh—bring light that shines to the world in darkness (1:5). Humanity has been penetrated by Kingdom culture in the form of a Man who models all that Heaven is. Though the darkness in man does not comprehend the light, the message is relevant to everyone, transcending any and every social and cultural barrier (1:9).

The message is able to transcend barriers because the messenger doesn't just speak; He models His message. The Word, Jesus, became flesh and dwelt among us (1:14). John conveys the sense of someone taking on not only the form of man, but his very nature. Jesus lived among us, not as a mimic parodying human behavior, but as a man in every sense of the word. This is the essence of modeling: incarnating Kingdom values while adopting the lifestyle of the target culture. In shedding His glory to become one with us, Jesus gave up an incredible amount. No wonder Paul describes Christ's attitude as one of sacrifice and humility. He was unwilling to hang onto what was rightfully His, but emptied Himself in obedience to take on the form of man. He actually became man.

Modeling seems to carry with it the responsibility of selflessness. This may be why there are so many poor models. Few are willing to pay the price of a new beginning, of changing what is comfortable for something different, not just outwardly but through and through. This transformation was so complete in Jesus that John tells us He was without sin in a manner that revealed grace and truth as we beheld His glory (1:14). Christ felt at home because He was home. He had made His home among us.

Do we enter the world of those we seek to serve and reach? Or do we ask them to enter ours? Do we model Kingdom values in our lifestyle among them, or do we exemplify tradition, our own cultural trappings, or social bias? This is not a way of saying tradition is unimportant, culture should be ignored, or social realities should be disparaged. Jesus did not consider these things unimportant. But neither did He allow them to obscure the clarity nor obstruct the mobility of the gospel. Furthermore, His life was without compromise with sin. We are called to live this way as well.

Jesus' Final Instructions

In chapter 7 we looked at Jesus' final instructions for His disciples. We were looking for His priorities—the core truths He wanted His followers to remember as they continued His work. Let's quickly review some of those core truths from a different perspective. A close look at His words and actions that evening can tell us a lot about what it means to model the gospel.

First, in washing His friends' feet, He modeled love and servanthood. Along with the example, He gave a new commandment: love one another (John 13:34). Why? So that mankind might learn from their example whose disciples they were (13:35).

The Master went on in John 14 to give reassurance, answering the kinds of questions we would be asking if we were there and feared being left alone. Change always brings difficult adjustments. Jesus had been the model; now He was leaving and they were to be models. That was a scary responsibility, but Jesus assured His friends that the Holy Spirit would be continually present to help them fulfill their role.

Even so, we are not perfect. So in John 15, Jesus laid out instructions for how to keep tapping into His power in order to do our job. Jesus wants us to abide in Him, to be concerned about healthy relationships with one another, and to maintain the right perspective about the world we have been left in to influence redemptively.

Some cautions were in order (John 16). Sometimes the way will not be clear, the going tough. We are not the Holy Spirit ourselves. Our role is to point the way to Jesus by what we say and how we live among the lost. We are messengers faced with the constant temptation to be convincers, arm-twisters.

Finally, Jesus passed on the reins of ministry and began to pray. What He prayed for is provocative.

Christ the Lord has manifested God, given His followers the Word, protected them, and given them unity. Now He sends them into the world with a prayer (John 17) that focuses on Himself, then His disciples, then His church. (How often have you heard you shouldn't pray first for yourself? Is this another ascetic tradition?) One of His concerns is that His Father would fully manifest the truth of who He is through what is about to happen. This is one aspect of Christ's ministry on earth—that of glorifying the Father—that is not usually considered in the context of modeling.

To manifest His name is in effect to reveal the nature of God's very character in what we say or do. This dimension of glorifying God—shedding light on the truth of who He is and the response He wants from mankind—is something we can accomplish through modeling the message of the gospel.

Jesus goes on to expand on the meaning of the gospel in an unusual way: eternal life consists of knowing Him, having a personal relationship with the living Son of God, Jesus Christ. This capsule of the gospel is so simple and straightforward that it can be modeled by anyone and can cross social or cultural boundaries without distortion.

Jesus recognizes that, apart from God, it is not possible for us to act in unity. Therefore He prays for the disciples' protection from the evil one, the world, and themselves. In expanding His prayer to include all those down through the ages who will believe, Jesus asks that they be dedicated to the Truth, spiritually reproduce their faith and, above all, maintain their unity. Why should the unity of the church be so important? It is one more evidence that Jesus is who He claims to be: sent by the Father to reconcile a lost world. Modeling love and unity, personally and as a Body, is one of the church's primary ministries.

A Philosophy of Ministry

The ministry of the church also involves relating the unchanging nature of the Word of God to the changing nature of the world as agents of the Kingdom. What enables this process is a philosophy of ministry. Every institution, every person has one—acknowledged, articulated, understood or not. It is what drives our modeling consciously and, more importantly, unconsciously. It determines how we do business, how we relate to people, how we carry out the mission.

A ministry philosophy consists of conceptual and practical elements: what we say and what we do. Congruence between what we say and do builds trust, while large differences build cynicism.

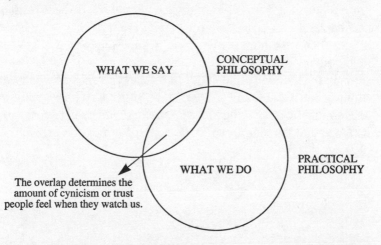

WHAT WE SAY

CONCEPTUAL PHILOSOPHY

WHAT WE DO

PRACTICAL PHILOSOPHY

The overlap determines the amount of cynicism or trust people feel when they watch us.

The process of contextualization is to make conceptual and practical philosophy of ministry congruent, and relate them to the real world in meaningful ways that do not compromise sound doctrine. In other words, what we say should match what we do and fit those we seek to serve and reach—all without sin. A tall order? Yes, but it is essential. Contextualizing our ministry requires us to continuously sift our methods—old beliefs, rituals, stories, and customs. Are they still meaningful, necessary, and relevant?

In the church, our conceptual philosophy (what we say)

may be biblical and relevant, while what we do may be quite different. In that case, we need to focus our efforts at changing our practical philosophy. We need to scrutinize our attitudes, core heart beliefs, characteristic ways of responding to people and situations, and driving values. Are they—the real forces behind our actions—truly biblical and relevant?

Taking a hard look at our practical philosophy is not easy. It's scary because we often don't enjoy discovering the truth about ourselves. We also find it hard to see ourselves clearly even when we want to. But this hard look is a crucial step toward an effective ministry. Community, which we'll discuss further in chapter 12, is invaluable for helping one another see what's really there. An honest invitation to the Holy Spirit to reveal and convict is also vital.

In reshaping a philosophy of ministry, we need to keep in mind what is fixed and what is not. A ministry philosophy is a response to two things: the *Word of God*, which does not change; and the *world*, which does.

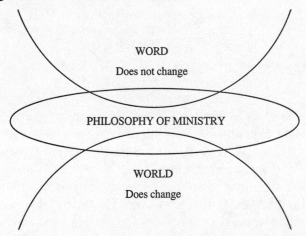

WORD

Does not change

PHILOSOPHY OF MINISTRY

WORLD

Does change

Knowing that the world changes but the Word doesn't, we need to beware of wrong responses to the pressures for fitting ministry to the audience (contextualization). One response is to simply deny the old patterns and forms. There is great risk in losing touch with transcendent, valuable elements—healthy traditions of ministry—by arbitrarily rejecting old ways. Equally dangerous is uncritically accepting old ways, for this leads to compromise. Whether syncretism results from not shedding things to be rid of or from undiscerningly incorporating the new, it is still death to the gospel message.

A ministry philosophy must integrate the old and the new under the critical supervision of the Spirit of God and the Word of God. Our modeling will simply reproduce error if we rely only on our training and conventional human wisdom. Contextualizing ministry is a process of understanding the original purposes of the old, examining the biblical teachings about the matter under scrutiny, evaluating the old in light of these teachings, and prayerfully creating a new practice.

Knowing Your Audience

Willow Creek, a large Illinois church, developed a contextualized ministry to the community in a natural process. The church wanted to reach the generation that grew up on television. Therefore, various services include drama, nontraditional music and programs, counseling, and a focus on relevant day-to-day issues from a biblical perspective. A newspaper article reported that what keyed the leadership of this church to opportunities with this generation was the response to door-to-door surveys conducted in the community they wanted to reach. The surveys revealed that people found church boring, predictable, and money-hungry. It is interesting to note that where Willow Creek's *function* of targeting the audience for contextualized ministry has been reproduced, similar effective ministries thrive. But where the *form* or pattern has been methodologically reproduced without effort to understand the audience, the church struggles.

Fellowship Bible Church, a large Colorado church, sought

from its inception to understand the community it desired to serve and reach. Within five years, it had to go to three services, not just to serve the Christians in the community, but also to serve the lost who were coming to Christ. Fellowship Bible's ministries, worship services, and programs were relevant to the spiritual and social needs of the audience. Yet its structure and activities look very different from those of Willow Creek because its audience is very different. Coloradoans and Chicagoans, even of the same age bracket, are not the same. Fellowship Bible is not reproducing a pattern or method; it is employing the principle of contextualization.

The key is in reproducing function, not form. Function is related to the larger purpose to be served. For example, edifying the saved and reaching the lost are functions of the church. Forms are the procedures, structures, activities, etc., that emerge to accomplish a function. Fellowship Bible and Willow Creek are committed to similar functions, but they use very different forms. The differences have to do with the audience, the social climate, the founding purposes of each church, and so on. Receiver-orientation dictates that, within the bounds of Scripture, the target audience to a large degree determines the form.

Leadership

Having a relevant philosophy of ministry and knowing the audience are the first two steps in contextualization. But they are inadequate unless accompanied by proper leadership. Leaders who influence change, motivate and mobilize the laity, and contribute to movement are different from leaders who direct hierarchic institutions.

Tim directed a large Christian ministry. This youth ministry had grown to include several layers of management, a large payroll, considerable facilities, and numerous programs. Tim's autocratic leadership style and strong, driving personality had served the work well in its nearly twenty-five-year history. But now he was facing the possibility of being relieved of duty. Relationships with the staff were poor; financing for the ministry was running behind; and the public interest in the ministry seemed to be declining.

When Tim and I (Jeff) discussed the situation, his feelings about what was wrong were very strong. "These kids we get for staff just don't respect their elders anymore! You would think because of my age and experience they might realize I have at least some spiritual authority," he complained. When I asked for some specific examples, Tim generalized. "When I want someone to do something, they need to jump to it, not argue with me. There seems to be too few faithful kids and too many lazy ones around. And they are so self-centered, not concerned about the program at all!"

Tim had missed something important. People have changed. These young adults hired as staff have a different set of values and norms than those he hired even five years ago. The shocks that have hit families in the last twenty years have left a generation that struggles with authority, mistrusts the generation that destroyed their homes, and views the world through more individualistic eyes. Tim not only ignored what had wounded these men and women, but was frustrated as well that they didn't recognize their rudeness, lack of respect, and demandingness as sin.

The problem lay in Tim's inflexibility and in his sinful demand to be totally in charge. His staff had deep relational and spiritual needs he was not responding to. He demanded loyalty and obedience from those with a limited capacity to respond. He did nothing to come alongside, encourage, affirm—earn their trust. Instead of helping them see how demandingness affects others, hurts themselves, and ultimately disappoints God, Tim just told them to "get out of sin." Tim needed to change his leadership style. But his commitment to the "program" and

104 / A Biblical Alternative

the requirements of running the institutional structure kept him from seeing the problem in terms of people and limited his ability to respond even if he did understand.

Perhaps eliminating some of the bureaucracy in his organization would have helped, both in administration and a level or two of management. Certainly someone needed to be in control, though, and the organization wouldn't function without an infrastructure. But the real problem lay not in the inflexibility and insensitivity of an institutional structure, but in the different generational expectations of Tim and his staff and the growing irrelevance of the ministry to the public. Their program-oriented, cookie-cutter ministry no longer sufficiently addressed real needs in the lives of today's youth. Therefore, parents lost interest in financially supporting the ministry. Other ministries offered better programs at less cost.

Because Tim failed to understand and adapt, he lost his job. The board replaced him with someone more in tune with the times. It is interesting that his replacement is just as driving, just as strong in personality, and just as much a "take-charge" person. However, these energies are channeled toward directing and influencing, not demanding and controlling.

Tim's training as a leader was typical. It included a rational, logical model of thinking, leading, and doing business. Tim became a detached, analytical leader, requiring justification for every decision.

Traditional leadership development in the church focuses on skills needed to ensure a stable and orderly institution. This tends to produce cool and aloof models who see management as control. Leaders of movements (the Kingdom is not an institution) do not control; they enable others. This leader's role is to take us to places we have never been before. It is a shared role, not heroic, lone-wolf individualism. Risky, innovative, and vulnerable, this kind of leader must be able to see the wide perspective, God's larger purposes, rather than just drive to accomplish immediate objectives. The wide view is crucial, not only because it keeps the leader from veering off course from God's agenda, but also because it enables him to frame differences and problems so that participants focus on what is to be gained by change rather than what is to be lost. This leader makes the intangibles of vision tangible through modeling, not mouthing, the redemptive difference change brings. Though directive when necessary, such leaders are primarily facilitators and influencers who enable others to do the job.

The Qualities of a Messenger
Change that does not destroy the ministry in the very act of bringing greater biblical relevance to it requires three things: an understanding of the audience; a philosophy of ministry that enables contextualization of the message for the audience; and the right kind of leadership to pull it off. On a more personal level, just what kind of person has what it takes to do this? What kind of messengers are the ones who must carry the message to the lost?

First, in word and action, our communication must cross social and cultural boundaries without warping the message. What we model and teach must be receiver-oriented. We have to deal with normal conflict and tensions constructively, biblically. Although communicating in the context of the hearer's realm has always been important, it is especially an issue today, when the church is relying on outdated paradigms of communication. Most evangelism strategies are proclamational: one proclaims the message verbally. Some people have supported friendship evangelism, incarnating the gospel in one's actions, as a better way. But what we need to do is sensitively apply both proclamation and incarnation in a manner relevant to each unique audience.

Christ's life reveals timeless principles that allow Kingdom values to permeate every society of every age. He was often addressed as "Teacher." This title balanced two realities fundamental to modeling. The teacher in Jesus' day was both the expert and example of his instruction. His life exemplified the teacher's lesson, whether the message was philosophy or a trade skill. As the Teacher, Jesus modeled His message. It is as if He acted intentionally to ensure that His actions would not obscure His message. He did this by incarnating the Kingdom values, adopting a lifestyle that did not compromise with sin, and displaying grace and truth in every action. The result: the model penetrated a culture and eventually ignited a movement, changing lives the world over.

In John 2:1-9, Jesus responds to a wedding invitation. His disciples and He participate in the celebration and Jesus miraculously supplies wine from water when the stock runs out. Some people try to interpret this narrowly as grape juice in an attempt to harmonize their doctrine with Scripture. It was not. Both historical study and the logic of the passage make clear that it was wine. Jesus and His followers partake of it rather than offend their host even though later in His ministry Jesus was accused of being a drunk. Though He never was a drunk, the rumor clearly had its roots in observed practices. The point is this: Jesus was different *in* His culture but not different *from* His culture. What kept Jesus from unbiblical compromise was that He balanced appropriate participation in life with not alienating Himself from those He came to redeem. This is the essence of receiver-orientation.

God is not troubled by the variety of cultures. In Genesis 12:3 He promises Abraham that in you all the families of the earth shall be blessed. God implies that cultural boundaries will provide no obstacle to His purposes. Accordingly, culture was no barrier for Jesus in accomplishing His ministry on earth. He became a Jew in every sense of the word, yet His ministry ignited a movement that transcended Jewishness and spread to "all the families of the earth."

To follow Jesus' example, we need an intimate knowledge of people and their norms and values. Our goal is to plant an idea—the gospel—in such a way that members of a culture can embrace it without distorting it, but also in a way that no culture can contain and claim ownership of it.

Speaking the Culture's Language

Just as we need to incarnate the gospel, we also need to understand social and cultural boundaries. Any audience is predisposed to attach skeptical or negative connotations to communication that appears to come from outside its cultural or social sphere without due regard to difference. An audience responds to a message that comes from within its sphere or has constructively affirmed and acknowledged the differences between its sphere and that of the message giver.

Communication, then, must be reciprocal if meaning is to be clear. We minimize or eliminate boundaries by interacting with our audience. Instead of preaching, assuming we've made ourselves clear, and leaving, we listen and observe, then speak in language we think the hearer will respond to. We then listen again to learn if we've been clear, then if necessary, clarify.

John 2:23–4:42 amply illustrates this dynamic. Jesus understood and used the language and culture of the target audiences. Consider first the Jewish Pharisee, Nicodemus. He was not only a Jew but a member of the ruling council (3:1). He approached the Teacher bound by protocol, tradition, and culture (3:2). In explaining the gospel, Jesus took care to use terminology and metaphors with which Nicodemus would identify (3:3). He let Nicodemus's responses influence the direction of the conversation and gave no hint of condemning what Nicodemus was or represented (3:4-21). As a result, He brought Nicodemus further along in his understanding of who Jesus was and what being "born again" was really all about.

Merely understanding spiritual truth is not enough to save.

But Jesus' receiver-orientation sowed the Word in a manner that did not abuse Nicodemus; Jesus gave Nicodemus the freedom to open up, respond, or even back away to think without pressure. The end of John's gospel suggests that Nicodemus later embraced Christianity at great personal cost. Jesus did not demand instantaneous commitment or response from Nicodemus. Jesus gave people time to change.

In chapter 4, we find the Lord leaving for Galilee (4:1-4). John the Baptist had been barely tolerated in Judea; Jesus made things worse. The Pharisees would have prematurely dealt with the situation had Jesus not chosen to withdraw before the fabric of that social setting was rent beyond recovery. Choosing to go through Samaria, He ran into a Samaritan woman. Though the Lord was clearly a Jew (4:6), a race hostile to Samaritans, His presence did not make her uncomfortable. As with Nicodemus, Jesus found a way to spark her curiosity and open a door for communication (4:10). Again, He dipped into the mindset of the listener to make His point, using statements and illustrations appropriate for the audience at hand (4:13-26). The audience, not a program, determined His approach.

Though Jesus did not reveal who He was to Nicodemus, He clearly did with the woman (4:26). Her prejudices were less blinding; the Pharisee would have reacted negatively to such explosive words as *Messiah* if Jesus had been that clear with him. Jesus did not expose the truth beyond the listeners' capacity to respond to it. His approach was effective; the woman's testimony to those of her own social class had tremendous impact (4:39-42).

How was He able to quickly adjust His interpersonal style? John 2:24-25 says of Christ, "He knew all men. . . . He knew what was in man." Jesus knew Himself in relationship to His audience, and He understood the mindset the gospel would have to penetrate. This is key to receiver-orientation. Jesus was where the people were, participating in their activities, coming alongside them in an understanding way. He molded His conduct and conversation to their social sphere of reference (John 18:20). He put His message into the context of their lives, and consequently, His proclamation affirmed His lifestyle.

Being receiver-oriented involves communicating in such a way that attention is not drawn to the communicator, for that would obscure the message. Rather, make every effort to meet the listener where he is. This means communicating with our lives as well as with words in the terms of the receiver's social setting and culture (1 Corinthians 9:22).

Learning to communicate to a particular audience will make clear what activities will facilitate ministry. Once we understand the language and have identified effective activities, it will start becoming clear how to organize for ministry. (This is the opposite of what most churches do today. We tend to start with a structure through which we thrust ministry upon the audience without regard to relevance.)

Language expresses behavioral patterns, attitudes, and perceptions inherent in the culture. As children learn speech, they also learn the requirements of their social structure. Learning to communicate across cultural and social boundaries also teaches us what the obstacles and opportunities for the gospel are in the new environment. What form the ministry should take will naturally suggest itself. As the audience changes, so will the form of ministry. Thus, a functional approach tied to communication rather than a structural approach tied to a form guarantees continuing relevance.

Confronting the Culture

Contextualizing the gospel involves more than the responsiveness of receiver-orientation. It also involves cultural confrontation. The incident with the Samaritan woman required that Jesus set aside some conventional behavior (4:27). A rabbi or teacher did not speak to women in the street. Jesus deliberately chose to break that cultural norm to convey His message. In fact, part of what caught the woman's attention was the shock of a rabbi breaking this custom. Jesus wasn't ignorant of His culture's rules, nor did He break them to suit His comfort. He kept them or broke them according to the need of the moment.

Receiver-orientation requires discerning which conventions to ignore and which to affirm in the culture. Inevitably, Kingdom values will force a confrontation between Kingdom culture and fallen human culture. In John 2:14-16, Jesus confronts the corruption of selling sacrifices and exchanging money in the Temple and alienates His audience in the process. How do we differentiate between valid convention and inconsequential convention? How do we deal with the inevitable tensions cultural confrontation generates?

In John 5:1-13, Jesus challenges another convention. The confrontation is premeditated (5:1-6). Jesus knows the history of Bethseda and the obvious answer to the question He asks the man who has been sick for thirty-eight years: "Do you wish to get well?" He asks the question for the benefit of the audience. Now, the day is the Sabbath, and conventional interpretation of the Law dictates that no work (including carrying your pallet) can be done (5:9-10). Fascinating: the Jews are so distracted by a social taboo that significance of the miracle totally escapes them!

The man who is healed does not know who Jesus is (5:13). But later in 5:14-19, Jesus purposefully identifies Himself and becomes the focal point of a Sabbath controversy. In this context, part of the message that Jesus is God's Son starts to become clear (5:18), and persecution results. (Modeling and receiver-orientation are costly, risky business.) In the discussion this confrontation generates, the full message of the gospel becomes clear (5:19-32) as well as the obstacle of the critics' own unbelief (5:33-47). Jesus has challenged a convention and risked a negative response in order to make clear the real issue (the gospel) and the real problem (pride, unbelief).

If a healthy response to the gospel involves being drawn to Christ (John 6:65) in a process of reconciliation, then any convention that impedes movement in a redemptive direction needs to be challenged. The manner of confrontation must take into consideration the nature of the audience, the nature of the message, and the nature of the overarching purpose of God. Daily life is filled with commonly accepted practices or conventions. Some are harmless, and we should be receiver-oriented enough to acknowledge and participate in them. Some can be modified and used as redemptive analogies. Others need to be challenged because they present obstacles to the gospel. However, we should make the challenge in a manner consistent with the culture and social circumstances. Jesus' balance in this is obvious in that although He had many critics, others obviously responded positively to Him (6:2). Discerning the difference in opportunities is a function of understanding oneself, the message, and the culture.

Timing
One way to reduce tension when confrontation is inevitable is to have a sense of timing that acknowledges the cultural setting. In John 7:1-2 we are told it is the time of the Feast of Booths, one of the three great festivals Mosaic Law required adult males to attend. Christ's brothers are pushing for a sign, even for a premature confrontation with His adversaries (7:1-5). Jesus risks being misunderstood by apparently violating the Law (7:9) in order to remain true to God's purpose. Timing is related to this purpose. For Jesus, timing is critical; for His brothers, it is not. Christ has different reasons for going than His brothers have for Him (7:3-10). Jesus times His arrival at the feast so that tensions are minimized and unnecessary confrontations avoided.

He begins to teach in the Temple (7:14), the accepted place

for this activity. A premature confrontation over nonessential issues would prejudice His audience. It would make them view His communication as adversarial, coming from outside their bias, an unnecessary boundary. As it turns out, Jesus' careful timing predisposes them to listen with openness (7:15). This, in turn, makes it possible to deal with an essential issue: a wrong basis for judgment, a selfish inconsistency in interpreting the Law (7:21-24). The responses that follow indicate that those with the most to protect are alienated, but others are drawn closer to the truth. If Jesus had lacked a sense of timing rooted in an understanding of the culture, no one would have come closer.

Jesus combines a sense of timing with a redemptive analogy when He challenges convention later in the Feast (7:37-38). The last day of the Feast involves a tremendous water ritual. Christ stands and shouts at just the right moment, "If anyone is thirsty, let him come to me and drink" (7:37). The clear implication is that Jesus has a better alternative to ritual. At any other place and time, this metaphor would have been nonsensical.

Sometimes there is no way to avoid confrontation or reduce tension. In John 8:12-20, we find Jesus in the treasury of the Temple. The treasury was lit by two colossal, golden lampstands on which hung a multitude of lamps. Christ's meaning did not escape His listeners when He said, "I am the light of the world" (8:12), referring to these lampstands. The rest of the chapter records a heated discussion centered on who He really is. Understanding no longer is the issue. Jesus aggressively confronts them only after the truth about sinful man and about who Jesus really is has been understood but rejected. There is a difference between challenging a convention and attacking character in bold confrontation. In light of their rejection, Christ condemns them (8:44-47).

Clearly, this kind of confrontation is the least preferred form of communication. However, it is His adversaries who escalate the verbal warfare, not Jesus. He was careful as well not to respond to the innuendoes used to provoke Him: calling Him a liar (8:13); twisting reality (8:33); questioning His illegitimacy (rumors of the virgin birth still circulated (8:41)); and calling Him dirty names (8:48,52). In all of this, there are those who believe (8:30-31), and to these He reveals another Kingdom value: "If you abide in My Word, then you are truly disciples of Mine" (8:31, NASB).

Man's culture is inherently blind (8:42-47) to the truth of the gospel. We need to develop a relevant understanding of the message in the context of that fallen culture as part of the evangelizing process. That process will bring the reality of God in Christ face to face with the bankrupt philosophies of the social order. That alone will create enough problems without our ineptness confusing issues further.

Confronting culture will necessarily involve challenging conventions that impede the relevant, accurate communication of the contextualized gospel. Challenging conventions will involve teaching that there are no alternatives to Christ. But we can convince people that there really are no alternatives only if our overall attitude is one of accepting them as people, with all of their cultural baggage. And we'll need a keen sense of timing in order to handle the tensions that arise.

PART THREE

THE DYNAMICS OF CHANGE

9

Biblical Leadership

C hurch success stories abound. We cited two examples in chapter 8: Willow Creek and Fellowship Bible. If the leaders of these two churches that experienced tremendous growth were to write "how-to-do-it" books, many aspiring leaders would try to follow their patterns and fail. Similar training, similar gifts, similar leadership styles produce radically different results. Why? The issue goes beyond the differences among audiences (which we've already discussed) and centers on what a biblical leader is, how God prepares leaders, and what a biblical perspective on growth is.

Helpless Dependence
One of the greatest illustrations of how God prepares His sovereignly chosen leaders is Moses. In Exodus 2:11-15, Moses tells us about the end of the first phase of his life. He saw an Egyptian beating a Hebrew, looked to make sure he wouldn't be caught, killed the Egyptian, and hid him in the sand. The next day he learned his deed was observed and reported to Pharaoh. He then fled and began the next major phase of his life in the wilderness.

Suppose that between verses 12 and 13 God visited Moses. He had just slain the Egyptian and didn't know he had been observed. What if God had said to Moses, "I'm going to lead your people out of this mess, and I need a great warrior to do the job. Moses, your intensity, fearlessness, and bravery impress Me, and I want you to be my man," how do you think Moses would have responded? I am convinced he would have enthusiastically said, "I'm ready; let's do it."

But God didn't ask him at that time. When Moses may have felt ready, God knew better. The zeal was there, but it needed refining. God then began his preparation for biblical leadership by nurturing him with forty years in the desert.

When his training was over, Moses' response to God's call was the direct opposite of what we would normally expect. In Exodus 3:7-10, God told Moses He had seen the affliction of His people, wanted to free them, and had chosen Moses to be their leader. But Moses didn't think he had what it took to do the job.

In 3:11 he began to shrink from the task. He continued to make excuses, and God continued to reassure him that He would be with him. Finally, in 4:13, Moses realized he couldn't reason God out of the appointment and pleaded that He send someone else. God became angry and partially conceded, allowing Aaron to be the spokesman, but would not let Moses off the hook. When God saw him as ready, Moses didn't feel ready. He felt helpless and overwhelmed. But through Moses, God directed a great movement.

God's process of developing leaders is radically different from ours. We want to make potential leaders feel ready with strategies, programs, and plans. God wants to strip them to helpless dependency on Him.

The Apostle Paul is another example of God's seminary education. In 2 Corinthians 12:1-10, we see God's hand in molding Paul. Paul recounts when he was caught up into

Paradise and given inexpressible information from the Lord. But even while receiving insights that might have made him feel self-confident, Paul was learning that it was not him, but God working in and through him, that made things happen. It was not his skills, intellect, management style, or a "how-to-do-it" book that got results. It was his weakness that enabled God to work in and through him.

Paul thought his "thorn in the flesh"—perhaps poor eyes, perhaps not—was holding him back from even greater ministry. God knew this was not the case. The thorn was to keep him dependent. As long as he knew he had severe limitations, then he would not exalt himself too highly.

We see here Paul's humanity. He didn't enjoy his thorn in the flesh. In fact, he entreated God three times to remove it. But God in His love did not grant his seemingly legitimate request.

Remember the doctor who had to inflict agony on his son in order to heal him. In the same way, God took Paul through severe pain as he developed his character. Paul knew that was where the full power of God is released. When I am stripped of control and am moved to helpless dependence, then God's power is released. Paul said he had learned a valuable lesson. When he wanted control of his activities to do greater work for God, He was deceiving himself. When control slipped away, active dependency resulted. When he felt weak, he was really strong in the Lord. What was foolish to man was the wisdom of the Lord.

The ultimate example of emptying oneself of power was Christ Himself. Jesus Christ, God in the flesh, emptied Himself of His sovereign power and became man. Circumstances crashed in on Him. From a human perspective, He was not much of a leader. His following diminished. He was crucified and gave His spirit into His Father's control. If you were living then, you would have assumed He was a colossal failure. But by emptying Himself, He made it possible for His Father to exalt Him, to reconcile His church, as the Father honored His Son's faithfulness.

Defining Success

Some years ago, I (Bill) was on a committee whose task was to define leadership. The prevalent thinking was to define it in terms of observed results. Unfortunately, we have become strongly influenced by the behavioral sciences, especially behaviorism, which deals only with external, observable data. So, this committee thought of leaders as the movers and shakers of people. This definition has some merit, but it has serious drawbacks.

By definition, a leader implies a following. So we train potential leaders in seminary to shepherd the sheep, to lead and have them follow. Men graduate, go to a church, see themselves as leaders, and expect the congregation to follow. After all, they are ordained of God to the position. When people don't follow, they read how-to books to get God to bless their ministry. Frustration, clearly not a fruit of the Spirit, can result when they feel themselves as failures when churches don't respond favorably.

What is really happening is that man is attempting to gain control of a congregation and looking for a nonexistent formula to make it happen. Perhaps this highly esteemed position of leadership the pastor has been taught to seek is becoming his driving force in life. Maybe the words of Christ recorded in Luke 16:15 apply: "You are the ones who justify yourselves in the eyes of men, but God knows your hearts. What is highly valued among men is detestable in God's sight." Maybe training men to be leaders and somehow gain control of their congregation is sinful.

But the fact remains that God has clearly called some to leadership. How, then, is it measured? Who is responsible for gathering a following? What is God calling us to do?

How do we measure the leadership of Moses, Paul, and Christ? If you were living during their lifetimes, you would have seen different observable data. With Moses, you would have seen failure, murmurings, suffering. Moses himself never entered the Promised Land. But you would have seen visible evidence of a large following, a following placed there by God and not dependent on Moses' control of the situation.

With Paul, you would have seen a very different situation. Paul planted churches and saw tremendous results during his journeys. But he also saw problems creeping into the churches he planted. Not only were they having problems, but his own limitations restricted his ability to face and resolve these problems. Because of the difficulties of travel and his periodic imprisonments, he was often restricted to writing letters. Toward the end of his life, his empire seemed to collapse. In 2 Timothy 4:16-18 he said, "At my first defense, no one came to my support, but everyone deserted me. May it not be held against them. But the Lord stood at my side and gave me strength, so that the message might be fully proclaimed and all the Gentiles might hear it."

Was Paul a leader even though the churches he planted were struggling and no one came to his defense? His following seemed to be declining, not growing.

Our Lord Himself saw His following decline almost to nothing. Even God the Father seemed to have forsaken Him. Was He a leader, a great mover and shaker of people? An observer who did not know the Old Testament prophecies about Christ would have thought this movement had ended.

Christ and Paul were the greatest human leaders ever, but the visible results of their faithfulness were not fully manifested until after their departure from this world. Then God blessed their faithfulness with a large and growing following.

In chapter 8, we pointed to two successful churches: Willow Creek and Fellowship Bible. By what standard do we call them successful? Off the cuff, the answer might seem easy: we know they are succeeding because they are big. If you visit them, you will find lots of people doing lots of things. But if you ask the leaders of those churches, they will insist that the target they are aiming at is not bigness. Both leadership teams are aiming to build vibrant disciples of Jesus Christ. Bigness, they will tell you, is a byproduct of (and perhaps a means toward) that end.

Is that claim a pious ruse? Are these leaders really building kingdoms and cloaking their ambition in altruistic language? Jesus instructs us to assess trees by their fruit. If we want to know whether Willow Creek and Fellowship Bible are really succeeding in turning secular people into servants of Christ, we can peer past their bigness and examine the lives of individuals and groups in each body. This is exactly the test these leaders dare to apply to their own labors.

But even here, the test of visible results may be misleading. Pastor Bob graduated from seminary with all the tools to lead. He had answers and solutions. But Pete and Ann weren't responding, and his leadership was threatened. He was measuring his leadership by visible results. Clearly, to be a leader requires a following. But the attempt to secure a following requires control over another person. Therefore, the aspiration to be a leader as measured by a desired response does not let God exercise His sovereign choice in whether or not we have a following that does what we want.

Control Versus Character

For example, consider the husband-wife relationship in a biblical marriage. As a counselor, I (Bill) repeatedly see husbands (including pastors and missionaries) who come to me complaining that their wives won't submit. I see men almost daily whose anger has turned to rage because they demand that their wives respect, submit to, and appreciate them. After all, they are in God's service, and their wives should recognize that fact and treat them better.

What arrogance! What blindness to Paul's instructions to love them as Christ loved the church! These men want—demand—a following. They want their wives to be like good hunting dogs: follow all their orders to the letter and be warm and loving at night. They are blind to the gross sin in their own lives and are pointing out the speck in their wives' eyes.

These men are accepting the responsibility for their wives' submission, something completely beyond their control, by demanding compliance rather than loving as Christ loved the church. Christ was primarily concerned with doing His Father's will. When His following diminished (John 6:60-66), He never changed direction, but entrusted the response to His ministry to His Father. By contrast, the husbands in this example are not responsible for their wives' response to their efforts; they are responsible only for obeying God, modeling Christ, and loving their wives, no matter the response. The wives' submission is not the husbands' responsibility.

How radical! How freeing! God does not hold us responsible for others' response to our behavior. He holds us responsible only for our own development of Christlike character. That's hard enough! To add to that the need to find a biblical prescription to control another's behavior will inevitably produce frustration, which is not listed among the fruit of the Spirit in Galatians 5. The result—a loyal following—is totally God's prerogative. The following we so deeply want, if pursued, is according to Luke 16:15 *sin*! God wants us to develop character, not control people. He is the change agent in this case; we are merely the instruments He uses.

Second Peter 1:1-11 illustrates this concept. Peter is addressing Christians who have "received a faith as precious as ours" (1:1), who can find grace and peace not by controlling others, but by deeply knowing Jesus Christ. He has given to us everything we need for life and godliness by knowing Him. His preparation of His disciples in John 13–17 involves knowing His love and modeling it to others even when circumstances are grim, pain is great, and no great results are visible. .

In order to escape the inevitable frustration and corruption that result by trying to find ways to make others respond to us the way we want, we must trust God's promises and participate in His divine nature (2 Peter 1:4). As we participate, we move away from the corruption of manipulating others (even for "good" reasons) and begin to develop the characteristics of Christlike character that Peter lists in verses 5-7: faith, goodness, knowledge, self-control, perseverance, godliness, brotherly kindness, and love. Leadership is notably absent from this list.

When we develop these personal characteristics, we are no longer unproductive. We are then modeling the character qualities of Jesus Christ and are working in harmony with His Spirit. We become facilitators of the one true change Agent: God Himself. Verse 9 says that if these qualities are not truly developing within a person, he is not understanding and developing his salvation. There is no growth. This type of change, character development, must come from within and be in harmony with the Spirit of God working in us. It requires far more than self-discipline and moral effort.

Peter wraps up this thought by stating if you are developing these qualities "you will *never* fail" (emphasis mine). The issue is not a great following or great results. The issue is developing personal character from the inside out. Results in others may or may not happen. They are God's prerogative.

James 3:13-18 strongly supports this concept. If there is envy and selfish ambition, we admit them and face reality. These attitudes are not from God. If failure to convince one's spouse or congregation to follow Christ produces other than the characteristics of 2 Peter 1:1-11 (or the fruit of the Spirit of Galatians 5:22-23), we must realize that we are living according to wisdom that is not from above, no matter how we attempt to explain or rationalize a growing frustration, anger, or rage. We are taking the results into our own hands and accepting more responsibility than God allows us to have. That is sin, and the emotions it produces are its evil symptom. Wisdom from above produces the peace of allowing the results in others to be His responsibility. Our responsibility is to develop character and actively model the love of Christ to others. God's job is to bring about individual and institutional change.

10

Institutional Change

C hange creates tension. At the time of writing this chapter, I (Jeff) was working with a national corporation that had become somewhat institutionalized. The desire of its leaders was to become more flexible in their business practices, more relevant to their market, and more in tune with the times regarding personnel practices. No, the company was not interested in the latest management fads. They simply recognized that they were losing market share through obsolescence caused by rigid and irrelevant practices.

Studying an Organization
The first thing we did was to study the organization's history. We looked at both the company itself and the nature of its particular industry. Whenever people associate together around a common cause or set of causes within a given social framework, certain patterns or cycles emerge. (The church is no different in this sense. It is affected by human behaviors like any grouping of humans.)

Having identified where this organization was on its pilgrimage toward obsolescence (without change, every organization will ultimately fail), we then undertook a study of its driving values. What made it "tick" the way it did? Although many values are inherent in an organization, not all of them are driving. An organization's character, reflected in its culture, is a compilation of driving values: organizational, social/cultural, personal.

We then looked at the driving purpose or mission of the organization and asked: Are these the values needed? Are they wanted?

How do you get a company to undergo fundamental value change, to move toward driving values that will actually help the company serve its purpose? Change in organizational character is required. This means people will have to change the way they think about work, compensation, each other, the mission—the list is frighteningly long. This process of change, or growth, creates distrust, anxiety, and a lust for self-preservation among those most significantly affected. I found this to be true in the company with which I was consulting, even among those most in favor of and committed to the growth. The parallels for the church are obvious.

The Courage to Change

We humans like clear direction rather than the risk of ambiguity when we move forward. It appears to be God's nature to require change, yet it is man's nature to resist change. How, then, do we cope during times of change?

When Israel left Egypt and was not yet a nation in the true sense of the word, the people lived for some time in a state of flux. Caleb stands out as one who responded in a unique and constructive manner to the very real pressures of the time. From his life come valuable lessons for living with change.

Caleb was one of the proven leaders among the people of the Exodus. Moses picked him as one of the spies to check out the Promised Land. God made clear the role of the spies (Numbers 13:2): They were to survey the land, but it was God's job to deliver it into their possession. Confusion of these roles would produce failure.

Change can be quite unpredictable at times. Efforts should be directed toward fulfilling God's designated roles and not toward controlling the process. Wrong focus can lead to confusion of roles. Confusion of roles will produce failure for the church as it did for the children of Israel.

As they spied out the land, the obstacles to receiving the promise became clear (13:28-33). Caleb, however, chose to focus on the promise, not the problem. The tendency, in times of change, is to focus on what we risk losing instead of what we potentially will gain. Therefore, faith and courage are two fundamental ingredients of leadership during change. At Kadesh (13:25-33), Caleb demonstrated moral courage; his faith did not waver. The other ten spies measured their strength against the problem and came up short. Caleb instead focused on the vision God gave him.

Joshua was the only one of the twelve spies to join Caleb in this perspective. The other ten chose to focus on their inability to take the land, which was not their role in the first place. They would not let God be God, and because they were leaders, the people listened to them. When leadership fails to have a vision, the vision falters (14:30-33). Those involved in implementing change must have a shared vision if there is to be any success at all in communicating ownership of that vision to others.

Change inevitably puts leadership under fire (14:4). At Kadesh, Moses' wisdom and legitimacy came into question. But Joshua and Caleb, in spite of the antagonism of the people, remained steadfast in their role. They were the spies; God was the overcomer. Their vision was clear; the Lord could do what He had promised. The people, however, were paralyzed by fear (14:9-10).

It is one thing to take into account wise consideration of the risks and liabilities associated with change so as to have awareness and preparation to cope. It is an entirely different matter to be so committed to present realities that fear of losing them paralyzes the very people who should be involved in change. Fear of such problems paralyzes the people.

Moses assumed the shepherd's role in all this as an agent for reconciliation (14:19). He knew that what God planned would come to pass (14:20-21). God would use these people or set them aside. His plans would not be impeded. This is helpful today as we consider Christ's commitment to His church. Those unable to change will be set aside if change is of the Lord. Indeed, only Joshua and Caleb lived to inherit the promise and to inhabit the land. At eighty-five, Caleb was still going strong (Joshua 14:11-12). He did not shrink from the rigors of battle, and he succeeded where others failed. His vision remained clear, and his calling never wore out. Caleb wholly followed the Lord.

Commitment to Movement or Institution

One sees in this illustration that Caleb's heart in the matter was different from the others (Numbers 14:24). He was wholly focused on the Lord—not self, not others, not obstacles. He was committed to a movement, not just a band of people. What lay behind the other ten spies' reticence and complaint about leadership was a fundamental unfaithfulness toward God (14:2,27,33). Caleb's example reminds us to be committed to a movement, not just an institution.

Because of problems in his organization, Caleb endured forty years of frustration and disappointment. The difference in being committed to a movement and not to an organization or institution is in how the vision grips you. Can you live with the predictable unfaithfulness of others? Does your vision enable you to focus on the promise of the future and not the problems of the present? Are you wholly focused on the Lord such that giving up is not an option? Perseverance will outlast the consequences of change.

Hierarchically structured organizations require change initiated from the top down. That is where the freedom to initiate exists at first and where the authority to provide and preserve creative freedom resides. Simultaneously, the perception of ownership must be developed from the bottom up, where people most need to develop trust. This requires a highly participative process where various elements of the organization mutually affect the outcome. The change agent must do his best to influence this kind of balance, but he cannot demand it.

Do our ministries genuinely serve others or just ourselves? Do we serve others to fulfill our ministry goals, or is our ministry plan to serve in ways others perceive as genuinely helpful? Do we measure success by the quality of the relationships produced, or by the quantity, size, or numbers associated with our programs? We cannot cause growth in ministry; that is the sole province of God (1 Corinthians 3:5-9, 2 Corinthians 5:16-19). At best, we can remove obstacles to growth, unfettering the Holy Spirit. We can add real value to ministry when the goal is not God's blessing but rather to be deserving of that blessing. Our role in influencing change is to be participants in the Kingdom, acting with wisdom and being led by the Holy Spirit.

Avoiding Institutionalization
Before looking at principles for organizational renewal for the Body of Christ, it will be helpful to understand more deeply this matter of institution and movement.

An institution is something established that has a somewhat permanent rule of conduct or government, something forming a prominent or established feature in social or national life. When someone refers to a group or function having become an institution, he is recognizing certain established patterns, laws, or regulations that further some purpose. Institutions face several challenges. As they acquire capital property (buildings, etc.) and develop programs, resources that used to support the furtherance of their purpose are shunted into maintaining. those properties and programs. Sometimes upkeep can become their downfall.

Institutions are characterized by *bounded set thinking*. That is, there are written or unwritten rules that define whether a person is in or out of line. Now policies, methods, expectations, and rules are not harmful in themselves. They can encourage movement in the right direction. "You shall not commit adultery" is an extremely helpful rule for a healthy society. But unhelpful boundaries for institutions include rigid policies, forms that have outlived their functions, expectations for uniformity and conformity, rules that impede rather than enable. Bureaucracy tends to force procedures, rules, guidelines, policies, etc., on people. "Succeeding," or at least staying out of trouble, depends on staying within boundaries or achieving certain criteria. It is true that organization is necessary; rules help us function. But they also reflect social and cultural realities. As reality changes, the organization must also change if the institution is to still accomplish its purpose. But institutions are fixed by definition—they don't change. The goal, then, is to avoid institutionalization, to avoid becoming so bound by rules and tradition that relevant change is impossible.

A company I (Jeff) was helping illustrates how institutions outlive their usefulness when they are committed to forms that no longer serve the function or purpose for which they were designed. In this case, the outmoded form was literally a form—a computer form.

This company struggled with an attitude problem. The representatives in the field were supported administratively by a national headquarters, but they felt headquarters was totally out of touch with reality. Further, they felt headquarters had the attitude that they were the ones to be supported by the field representatives, not the other way around. A computer form became the focus and symbol of this controversy.

Headquarters used a complicated form to handle financial transactions for field representatives. The form was so complicated that many field people couldn't figure out how to use it, and mistakes often resulted. When someone suggested that a new form be designed, the representatives were told that this form was the one preferred by the data entry people in accounting. It was argued that satisfying the desires of a few clerks was not worth frustrating hundreds of representatives. Headquarters responded by saying 5,000 forms had been printed, and policy dictated using them until they were gone. Then a committee would look into the matter.

As I checked into this matter, I discovered that the form was actually unnecessary. The clerks found this form equally frustrating and long ago changed their procedures. The form had ceased to serve the function it was designed for. Yet, there was stubborn, institutional commitment to its preservation.

The church faces the same challenges. Its purpose is to be in the world for the lost, not for itself. Yet it consumes its resources primarily on itself and often does not recognize when its forms, programs, activities, traditions, and rules no longer accomplish their purpose with the audience.

Becoming a Movement

A movement is the rapid spread of an idea right for its time, usually in response to clear need. The Body of Christ needs to be propagating movement, not establishing institutions. This takes *centered set thinking*. That is, the set is defined not by its boundaries or rules, but by its focus or purpose. Movement (motion) and direction are important to centered set criteria. Is progress toward the goal in the right direction and in the right amount? Rather than looking at the number of verses memorized, one focuses on the qualitative changes resulting from an individual's efforts to bind the Word on his heart. (Scripture memory is only one of many constructive ways to encourage this.) Rather than counting baptisms, professions of faith, or cars in the parking lot to measure numeric growth, one looks to spiritual growth in support of benevolence, missions, outreach, and expanding interpersonal relationships within the congregation for a sense of progress. Fruit of the Spirit, character growth, and collaboration in community become measurement criteria, replacing budgets, positions, and numbers.

How can something institutionalized shift and become movement-oriented? How can an organization bounded by rigid rules, concepts, or traditions become unencumbered without losing what is necessary and valuable in those rules, concepts, and traditions? How can ministry provide the organization necessary to maintain order in chaos, yet at the same time create the opportunity for chaos amidst order? Answering these questions requires a process of organizational renewal. They are answered as you move ahead, not before you begin. This change process takes risk, and risk is antithetical to control-oriented people and institutions. We have no choice but to repent of the lust for control.

Organizational Culture

Organizational culture, a new buzz word in the business world, really applies to any group of people gathered around a common mission, purpose, or vision. The church has its own organizational culture that reflects not only its spiritual nature, but its denominational history, doctrine, social mores, and so on. Organizational culture, like a mirror, reflects the underlying character and driving values of the group—the environment. To influence change in organizational character, one does not focus innovative strategies on the organizational culture itself any more than a person, displeased with his reflection in the mirror, seeks to change his face by painting the mirror. A change in culture is achieved by a change in underlying character.

The interplay between culture, character, and driving values can be seen in Church XYZ. One expression of the corporate culture of this local church is the control used to maintain the quality, efficiency, and production of its programs and ministries. This control stems not only from the business model of management the denomination has bought into, but the "look good, maintain control" philosophy of the seminary training of the pastor and his associates as well as the director of Christian education and music director.

Although organization and control can be admirable and required qualities, this control is applied in an insensitive and autocratic manner. Supporting this environment of unhealthy control are several traits that together contribute to the corporate character of Church XYZ. It is located in a part of the country, for example, that typically displays a low opinion of the abilities of women. In addition, some key lay leaders behave in a manner only another prima donna could love. The leadership of this church values personal control and male dominance in an environment that encourages authoritarian excesses. These few driving values (both organizational and personal) have set the character of this church.

The point of examining Church XYZ is that if the person who wants to influence change tries to influence corporate culture directly—namely, the debilitating autocratic control—he will be ignoring the very characteristics feeding that culture trait. He would be addressing the symptoms and not the problem, and the corporate culture would not actually change. Remember, corporate culture is a reflection of underlying organizational character, which in turn is composed of characteristic ways of responding. These character traits are usually a composite of driving values: organizational, social, personal.

↗ CORPORATE CULTURE
↗ ORGANIZATIONAL CHARACTER
↗ CHARACTER TRAITS
DRIVING VALUES

Change Agents

Once thorough study has revealed the true corporate character, we can try to act as change agents. Change is not fundamentally predictable or controllable. Therefore, change agentry is as much art as science because, as with Church XYZ, not all problems within an institution are due to its culture. Some are more fundamental, the results of values and traits that are woven into its very character. The rules, guidelines, and principles of change agentry (which comprise its science) and the leadership, influence, and timing (which are art forms) are the subject of another book. But here it is important to note that the new does not replace the old instantaneously. Indeed, the old shouldn't necessarily be replaced at all.

People usually become aware of the need for new paradigms, for change from the old way of doing things, at the same time the old way of doing things is having its most success. Paradoxically, the need for "new" isn't apparent to forward-lookers until accomplishing the "old" no longer presents a challenge. Change agentry, then, must introduce the "new" without devaluing the "old," especially since something of the "old" may always be needed.

In reality, it is out of the "old" that the resources to drive the "new" are provided. Those who view the "old" as highly successful will naturally resist new things. Those who welcome change because they are looking to the viability of future ministry will resist the weight of old patterns. A good change agent accommodates both realities. History is filled with wave after wave of "new" things that have taken their natural place, only to be eventually replaced. In the Kingdom, these changes should be cause for joy, not strife.

11

Individual Change

In arrogant self-confidence, the Apostle Peter declared to
Jesus: "Even if all fall away on account of you, I never
will" (Matthew 26:33). Jesus' response was, *Not only will
you disown Me, but you'll do it three times before the night
is over*—a statement Peter immediately denied. But true to
Christ's prediction, Peter denied the Lord three times. When
he realized what he'd done, he wept bitterly. He had failed to
measure up to his commitment.

Coping with Failure
Peter was tormented by his failure to measure up to his boastful
statement of perfect commitment. The Lord used this situation to mold Peter's perspectives and move him closer toward
maturity.

In John 21:15-17, Jesus asked Peter, "Do you truly love
me more than these?" The word for love that Christ used
involves an act of the will, a commitment. He followed this
word with a comparison: Are you genuinely committed to Me
more than these (probably the other disciples)? But having
just boasted and failed, Peter backed off from the stronger

word and responded that he had a deep affection or fondness for Christ.

Jesus then restated the question without the comparison but still with the stronger word: "Do you truly love me?" Once again, Peter responded with the word that reflected a deep affection, not a brash commitment. Jesus' third question used the word Peter used: "Do you have a deep affection for me?" Peter's response was again the same.

Peter had learned a precious lesson. He had promised perfect commitment and had failed. He was unwilling to make the same statement again. He felt weak, unable to measure up to the standard he had so arrogantly set for himself only days before. But after each of Peter's replies, the Lord told him to minister to His sheep. Peter's failure softened his arrogance and brought him to active dependence. He became truly qualified for ministry by being humbled just as Moses was humbled for forty years in preparation for his mission. When God knew he was ready, Moses didn't feel ready. When Peter was ready, he, too, didn't feel it!

Pastor Bob (chapters 3 and 4) thought he was ready for ministry. He had been trained primarily with an infusion of information, a few ministry skills, and a code of Christian conduct. His situation was very similar to Peter's. He knew some facts, felt a high level of commitment, and believed that through moral effort and self-discipline he could measure up.

Both Bob and Peter were concerned more with behavioral change than with a deep change in perspective. But God knows our behavior will never measure up to His standards. What we began in the Spirit requires more than moral effort and self-discipline. We have seen how Peter was humbled. Pastor Bob, too, is beginning to fail. He is beginning to realize that life is beyond his control, and that he has neither a remedy for the ills in his church nor a proven program for growth. Failure is preparing him for active dependence—faith!

Rejoicing in Suffering

Paul states a surprising principle in Romans 5:3-5:

> We also rejoice in our sufferings, because we know that suffering produces perseverance; perseverance, character; and character, hope. And hope does not disappoint us, because God has poured out His love into our hearts by the Holy Spirit, whom He has given us.

It is rare for a Christian to say he is rejoicing in his suffering because it is molding his character. Instead, we see suffering as did Job's "comforters": "If you had just measured up, then you would be free of the agony you're going through. So dig out the sin, confess it, repent from it and go on with life." This is totally contrary to Christ's message in John 13-17.

The Lord says "expect suffering." We need to learn to respond to it as He would. As we do, we not only develop His character, but we also build pockets of communities as witnesses to Him (John 17:22-23). This process is spiritual; it is not under our control, nor are we even fully aware of what is happening to us. Exodus 34:29 records that Moses "was not aware his face was radiant because he had spoken with the LORD." In the same way, while others watch us become transformed into people who reflect the Lord's glory, we may not notice that we are doing anything more than continuing, by faith, to put one foot in front of the other. Now and then we'll catch a glimpse of our slow growth in Christ, and rejoice.

In Romans 5:3-5, Paul is building on Christ's message in John 13:17. Expect suffering; it strips you of control and forces dependence. Active dependence on Christ enables us to persevere in a world where relationships, vertically with God and horizontally with men, have been destroyed by sin. As we persevere, we develop character—predictable behaviors based on a supernatural perspective of the world we live in.

It is the development of character that produces hope. But what is our hope? Success? Great churches? Submissive wives? Loving husbands? Godly children? No!

Consider parenting. I (Bill) have been asked many times how to resolve problems with children. Typically, the child is from fourteen to sixteen years old, and rebellious behavior is beginning to surface. The parents are extremely frustrated and complain, "The harder we try, the worse he becomes." Parents feel helpless and hopeless.

The fact is that they are helpless. There is no series of behaviors that will change their children. The issue is how they persevere and develop Christlike character in response to the situation. When they begin that process, then their perspective can change. They are not responsible for producing godly children. They are responsible for being godly parents. When they pursue their own growth, they give control of both their growth and their children's over to the sovereign God. Then the Spirit of God can work in and through the parents as they love, become involved, teach (especially through modeling), and discipline.

This is not a "let go and let God" philosophy. It is one of letting go of what we can't control while actively modeling Christlike attitudes and behaviors. It is accepting and clinging to what is our responsibility before God.

The hope that Paul is talking about is not that our world would work according to our expectation. It's far more likely that it won't! The hope is an increasing assurance of God's sovereignty in all aspects of life—even the final outcome of our children's growth and maturity, even the size of the churches and businesses we oversee. But the journey to hope is an excruciating process as we are driven to prayer and God while our children (or churches, or businesses) seem headed toward certain destruction.

We tend to equip for ministry by the accumulation of

facts, which give us a sense of control. God equips for ministry through trials, tribulations, and failure—the agonizing but only way He can teach us active dependence.

Helplessness and Responsibility

Ann (chapter 3) was an innocent victim of physical and sexual abuse. She was conceived in lust, was a burden to her mother and an object for perverted sexual gratification by her step-father. Her pastor prescribed seemingly biblical behaviors to remedy the situation, but she never complied with them. How does someone like Ann move from efforts to comply with good behavior toward active dependence? She clearly has trials and tribulations to contend with during her growth process.

Ann is part of an ever-growing segment of the church today. Consequently, church leaders must have a philosophy of ministry that describes how God brings about change in people and how we should bring Scripture to bear upon our decadent culture. Just telling people, "Change your behavior" isn't having much, if any, impact.

Simplistically stated, there are two basic approaches in the church today for dealing with people like Ann. One position states that the past is under the blood of Christ; that fact should be accepted, and the individual should behave as if it's true. End of problem! The other extreme says that sin is under the blood of Christ, but that fact doesn't change the damage done by the abuser. Therefore, healing must take place. But questions remain. At what point is Ann healed sufficiently to live life? And to what degree is the church responsible for her healing before she can act responsibly?

On one side, we are asking Ann by an act of her will to remove the influence of a past where love has never been modeled or felt. But people like Ann often see our demand for compliance as a condition that she must meet in order to be accepted. Our demanding attitude does not appear significantly different from that of her abuser. Only the terms of the demands seem different to her.

But on the other side, we may be giving her an excuse for continuing learned, sinful patterns of behavior because her self-image isn't yet good enough. If she's not responsible to treat others with love until she's "healed," she may find it convenient to take a long time in healing. If she can count on being coddled, listened to, and excused because of her past suffering, she may be in no hurry to become whole.

Between these two extremes lies the center of biblical tension: the tough but necessary balancing act of understanding and promoting both obedience and healing. While we will be using Ann and her background as an example, the process is similar for most people even though circumstances and severity may differ.[1]

A Human Perspective

When Ann first sought help, she felt like a helpless victim of her circumstances. Life seemed to be out of control, as it has been since her earliest memories: a drunken stepfather whom she couldn't avoid and a mother who didn't protect her. The only resources she had ever learned were escape, avoidance, and denial.

Another common reality for Ann and others like her is self-contempt and personal shame, attitudes she has brought into her adult life to serve a distinct purpose. If she is a second-class person, she has an excuse to avoid life and keep all her relationships on a surface level—a sinful but understandable lifestyle. Her goal in life is not selfless ministry but self-protection from more pain.

As another person enters into her life to hear her burdens and model the love of Christ to her, deep emotions will begin to surface. She'll probably begin to feel personal guilt and worthlessness. At this point, many Christian counselors attempt to build a positive self-image, while completely ignoring two crucial ingredients of real change. The first is the deep sinful strategies Ann has developed to protect herself from pain. Ann must eventually face these if she is ever going to become whole and Christlike. The second ingredient is the cleansing she can receive when she understands Christ and His healing power. Only when Ann faces the depth of *her* sin—not just the ways in which she's been hurt, but also the loveless ways in which she has dealt with God and others—will she be driven to long for Christ's cleansing. But only when she encounters the crucified and resurrected Lord as a Person will she become free from the crushing guilt of that lovelessness. The error of the self-image approach to counseling is that it frequently sees the atonement as an act to make us feel worthy rather than as a necessity because of our utterly sinful condition.

Under the feelings of guilt and personal worthlessness is rage. When Ann feels this, her awareness of having been a victim will surface, and she will direct rage not only at the perpetrator but also at all those who had opportunities to rescue Ann and didn't come through. She will probably begin to put intense pressure on her pastor or whomever is befriending her at this point. No one else has ever come through for her. "You are God's agent to rescue me from the past" will be Ann's message to her newfound "savior."

I (Bill) have talked to men and women who have reached out and have found themselves in this position of savior. They either give in to all the demands or retreat from further involvement. Ann's rage will intensify and will be directed at the person attempting to help as he or she doesn't respond to the impossible demands.

This is a critical point in the process of helping Ann. Her past is a fact! The pain of the past will never be fully erased this side of Heaven, and the sad truth is that Ann must face her pain, knowing it will not vanish. Previously, she handled it by avoiding people or performing according to expectations. "Christian" behaviors enabled her to receive the approval of others. But now that she knows the pain will not totally disappear no matter how well she performs, her rage will intensify. Now she must face the fact that she has developed sinful strategies to cope with life. She must begin the process of confession, repentance, and acceptance of the grace of God. The beginning of accepting responsibility is to shift from angry victim to active dependence on God as a responsible child of God.

This process, as briefly summarized here, has several important characteristics. First, it is a process. If it were merely an act of the will, then self-discipline and moral effort would suffice. But it rarely, if ever, does. Peter's self-effort didn't last. Paul couldn't, by an act of his will, get rid of his thorn in the flesh that seemed to hinder his ministry. He wanted God to remove it, but God knew that Paul's thorn promoted dependence and growth. To remove it could make him feel self-sufficient. Paul's thorn, no matter how grievous or painful, was in his best interest!

Second, the process seems to always involve some level of pain as we are molded into Christ's image. Job, Jeremiah, Joseph, and Christ Himself suffered agony. Ann wants—demands—freedom from pain, but God doesn't promise escape from pain in a sinful world. He asks us to respond to it as Christ did.

Finally, we must become more and more aware of God's perspective when we encounter the painful aspects of life. Job became painfully aware of earthly reality before he was willing to accept God's perspective on life. When God allowed Satan to strip him of his family and wealth, Job seemed to accept God's providence with proper submission. But before God confronted him, he entered into rage and hopelessness. Only then was he ready to face ultimate reality: God's ways are not our ways. He has no obligation to make Himself fully understandable or to make us comfortable.

Awareness of the past and realization of our present helplessness open the door to dependence and hope. "I have told you these things, so that in me you may have peace. In this world you will have trouble. But take heart! I have overcome the world" (John 16:33).

Knowing that we are helpless but that trials do not affect a hope based on the Person and work of Christ is the basis for our faith. Stripped of ourselves, we must live by faith. There is no other valid option.

Active Dependence

Up to this point, it might seem that God is a sadist, allowing and inflicting pain at His whim. But we must realize that pain is a result of sin, and God is not the author of sin. So what is He up to? Why does He allow sin and suffering to play such a vital part in the process of sanctification?

Is it God's part of the process merely to make us miserable, to force us to depend on Him? No, God controls the whole process. When we discussed institutional change, we saw that God is the change agent and that we are not responsible to change anyone but ourselves. Likewise, if God is the change agent, then the process of individual change is beyond our capability also.

In chapter 7 we talked about the transformation described in Romans 12:2. A radical transformation—a metamorphosis—must take place, but it is far beyond our ability to attain by trying harder. We can't measure up no matter how hard we try. If we could, we would not be dependent beings. But by facing our powerlessness, we are forced into dependence, and then God's power can be released.

If it were possible for us to face our powerlessness without going through frustration and anguish, God would probably use an alternate route. But we are stubbornly committed to self-sufficiency, and few of us let go of our proud rebellion without being backed into corners repeatedly. God knows just how much it will take for each of us to stop waving our wooden swords around and let Him run the universe.

It will at times feel like we are living sacrifices (Romans 12:1), and we will want to crawl off the altar. But, like Peter in John 6:68, we must ask this question: Do we have a better alternative? Then we can say with Paul in 2 Corinthians 12:7-10 that God's power is released through our weaknesses. We can learn to be content with less-than-ideal conditions because we know they enable God to work in and through us.

Our responsibility is not to let our own agenda—a big church, spiritual children, prosperous business—get in His way as He works in us. Our attitude is not "let go and let God," but "let go of my agenda and diligently seek His agenda" as we let Him mold our character into Christ's likeness, as we learn to build Christian community by learning to love as He loves.

NOTE
1. For a detailed description of the change process, see *Understanding People* (Zondervan Publishing House, 1987) and *Inside Out* (NavPress, 1988) by Lawrence J. Crabb, Jr. For the process as related to abuse, see *The Wounded Heart* (NavPress, 1990) by Dan Allender.

12

Community Again

Defining the Product

Several years ago, I (Bill) was part of a discussion group that consisted of the elders of a church of 200-250 members. The church was in flux, and this group of men was charged with oversight and leadership to weather the difficult times. One of the elders, a successful businessman, said, "If this church were a business, we would be on the way out." Discussion followed as to how we needed to implement sound management practices for the church's survival.

This conversation triggered some questions in my mind. Are churches and businesses similar? How? Are they different? In what ways? Where do leaders of those organizations turn for guidance? Clearly, Scripture is the final authority for the church. But to what degree do business principles apply? And for the Christian businessman, how much of Scripture is relevant?

The last question is not directly related to the subject of our discussion, but Christ's admonition to "seek first his Kingdom and his righteousness, and all these things will be given to you as well" (Matthew 6:33) clearly tells the businessman what is

147

primary in God's sight. Modeling Christ's character is far more important than profit, from God's perspective.

How is the church uniquely different from a business organization? A business exists to produce a product. Without a product (be it a service or material goods) that produces a profit, the business would not survive. Although many businesses are beginning to pay more attention to the human resources involved in producing a product, the fact remains that without a product that is marketable, people are expendable. We see this fact daily in newspaper reports of layoffs in certain industries and areas of our country.

In the local church, the "product"—or more precisely, the aim—is to promote and facilitate growth of people toward Christlikeness. That's a real challenge in today's culture. Recently when I was speaking to several pastors, one stated, "It's very important that we have people of your training [counseling] to help people so the pastor and his staff can get on with the work of the church," which he saw as preaching, evangelism, choir, and so on. He was looking at people as resources to perform functions, not as men and women who were supposed to grow in Christlikeness.

The radical change in our culture over the last fifty years is making it even harder for us to help people become like Christ. When I was a child in the 1940s, the Judeo-Christian value system was given at least general approval, if not wholehearted support. But today, thanks to modern psychology, this value system that our country was founded on is seen as the problem, not the solution. People today are trying to make life work by using human reason alone, by trying to gratify all desires, and by releasing sinful passions to their fullest. The result is that our churches are full of people like Ann and Pete reaching for meaning and purpose in life. What they hear is simplistic: get busy for God and produce a product—new converts, beautiful music, or whatever.

Looking for Answers

As a culture, we are desperately searching, trying to make sense out of life and "be happy." We in the church erroneously assume that if we get busy for God, happiness will happen. But it all too frequently doesn't, so many church people are sent to therapists to get fixed so they can come back and perform. That is not God's design.

To make sense out of life, we have only two options. We can try to figure it out through personal experience or we can look for an outside authority. It is a major challenge these days just to consistently choose against personal experience. Then we have to sort through all of the outside authorities clamoring for our attention (including the traditions of this or that denomination). But when we correctly see Scripture as the singular outside authority, we find three broad categories to begin our evaluation.

First, we see the sovereign God at work to achieve His ultimate purpose. Although it remains in part a mystery, we see that He is bringing all things—the universe, the angelic world, humanity—together in Christ either for eternal glorification or destruction.

Second, we also discover that God has a universal purpose for all humanity: to come to know Christ and model Him to a lost world. We are to know Him, become like Him, and model Him.

Finally, each of us is to find our unique place in His ultimate objective—in church, industry, family, nation. We will never receive His praise for making a profit. We will receive His praise and reward for uniquely contributing, based on gifts and talents, to His sovereign master plan.

Individual in the Group

Our country is intensely individualistic. The Judeo-Christian value system is constantly under attack, and an attempt is underway to systematically destroy it, leaving people with no guidelines or values. The lie behind this movement is tolerance and freedom. But this view of freedom is producing anarchy, which removes freedom and destroys community. Individuals are left to fend for themselves according to their individual rules, goals, and desires. Community disintegrates, and without community—horizontal relationship based on vertical realities—man is less than he was designed to be.

How can we develop Christian community as God asks us to do? In the larger secular community, laws are made and ignored even by those who make them. Chuck Colson stated, "Societies are not held together by rules and laws; order cannot be enforced by swords and guns alone. People must find their motivation and meaning in powerful ideas—beliefs that justify their institutions and ideals."[1] What a powerful concept! Scripture is full of "powerful ideas," radical ideas that we in leadership have to more effectively communicate. But the process of communicating these ideas is increasingly difficult as we work with people brought up in a culture that sees truly biblical ideas as archaic at best and destructive to the human psyche at worst.

So people enter our churches with huge built-in barriers to genuine community. They've never seen it, and they've been taught to mistrust it. According to the propaganda, community means uniformity, oppression, control. Their childhood experiences of family community reinforce their fears of being controlled and exploited either by force or by emotional blackmail.

Then they sit in church and we tell them to get involved and perform for God. But they see their acceptance in the group as based on performance, and they rarely feel the love of God modeled in a deeply loving, committed community of believers. Acceptance appears conditional and shaky, no different from what Pete felt from his father and Ann felt from her abuser.

God calls us to something entirely different from this. He calls us to community based on the supernatural love of Christ. Acceptance in God's community isn't based on performance. If it were, we would all be in trouble. Only the finished work of Christ makes us acceptable. That fact makes the process of sanctification possible. For many people, the first step of sanctification is to feel Christ's acceptance as modeled through His children as they bear one another's burdens, weep with those who weep, and share one another's joy. This atmosphere allows an individual's uniqueness to surface as he begins to develop his or her gifts in service to God's sovereign purpose.

I (Bill) have observed a pattern in large churches pastored by men with unique gifts of preaching and teaching. The number of attendees remains high, but church rolls change constantly as people seek churches that will "meet their needs." Now, seeking to have needs met is not a biblical perspective. But to be aware that we are needy and to reach out to others at the level of the "needs" they feel is biblical. One of these "needs" (I prefer "legitimate longings") is to feel that one belongs to something larger than oneself. More particularly, we long to really *belong* to community, even when we don't know what that means. But a preaching service, while it can be an effective means of transferring information, will never satisfy that longing to belong. People remain isolated members of an audience.

We long to belong because God has designed us to live in community, in personal relationship with one another where His love is modeled. Personal relationships will not flourish because of formal preaching services, or even because of highly entertaining, modern-style services. If we want real community, we will have to do something else in addition to audience services.

The early church vividly modeled community. Acts 2:42 describes the people meeting in homes for fellowship, study, prayer, and the Lord's Supper. But establishing small groups won't work without biblical leaders who are aware of people in process, can lead the groups based on the needs of the moment, and can teach at where people really are. Some will need to be admonished, some encouraged, and some picked up and carried (1 Thessalonians 5:14).

Leaders must know their people and be able to teach Scriptures relevantly to individual lives. For a family who has just lost a child, Romans 8:28 is true but not appropriate at the moment. Putting into practice the love of Romans 12:9,14 by bearing this family's burdens is appropriate. Scripture addresses every aspect of life, but it takes wisdom to understand and apply it. *Wisdom* is the appropriate use of knowledge.

The Servant Leader

Leadership is vital! But what is biblical leadership? How can a leader motivate people to be a part of community and develop uniquely within the group?

First of all, a leader needs to understand what makes people tick, and in particular, what they need. He needs to understand people not according to the world's views, but according to the Scriptures. Christ knew what people needed. Above all else, they needed to face their sinfulness, and He provided for this need. He didn't just throw their sin in their faces (a tactic guaranteed to produce defensiveness). Nor did He indulge them. He discerned exactly what action He should take with each unique person to draw him to humble himself before God.

Leaders are not bosses. Leaders are those who initiate action, who take risks, who aren't afraid of failure. True leaders have an eternal perspective on life, no matter the immediate circumstances.

Leaders are those who are willing to look at Christ's call to continue His movement; who look at culture; who look to Scripture to seek God's perspective on how to reach a changing culture. They see the need to build a radical subculture within a decadent broad culture and to help men and women become a part of and grow in this subculture.

A leader sees that people in our culture are increasingly the products of broken families and perverse backgrounds that nourish a self-centered approach to life. Therefore, such a leader directs his teaching to people's desperate need of God's love and forgiveness. His deep concern is that they taste Christ so deeply, even in the midst of their difficulties, that they are inwardly motivated to bring others to know Christ.

Some time ago a pastor approached me who had just had an attendee at his church threaten suicide. His immediate reaction was to present the gospel. But it wasn't received, and the pastor admitted he had no idea what to do next. Even if the person had "prayed to receive Christ" (which may or may not have been a true conversion), what would come next? Is this person's problem resolved? If the person is truly converted, does this mean an end to the struggle with suicide? Is the pastor's job finished? I think not. Salvation is merely the beginning of change. It makes change possible, but Scripture must be taught to the person so that it is personally relevant. Relevant teaching requires that a pastor invest thought, time, prayer, and willingness to change both personally and professionally.

The leader must continually attempt to balance ministering to people who have been victimized with dealing with them as responsible adults. He remembers that their baggage didn't disappear when they became believers. One of his main objectives is to integrate people into a biblical community, where ongoing nurturing can take place. The leader doesn't expect himself to be everything to someone that a whole community of God's servants should be. Instead, he equips a community to serve the spectrum of functions for each other.

Above all, he consistently models the fruit of the Spirit in his own life as a true disciple of Jesus Christ.

Plurality of Leadership

It is clear that the church, the Body of Christ, is to have leadership (Hebrews 13:7,17). Organization is not wrong or carnal. However, people go to extremes on this matter. Some feel the less organization the better, but their work is often hindered because they lack sufficient organization. Others go to the other extreme and are so highly organized that it is difficult, if not impossible, for Christ as the Head of the church to be heard!

The New Testament does sanction several classes of leaders: bishops, elders, and deacons. Selection of these leaders in the earliest life of the church appears to have been a combination of an inward call by the Holy Spirit, an external call by the church, and "ordaining" to the office by the apostles.

In reality, the biblical evidence suggests that elders and bishops are the same people. These two names are associated with the same office (Acts 20:17,28; Philippians 1:1; Titus 1:5,7). The office of bishop as we know it today did not come into being until after the end of the apostolic age in the second century. Elder (presbyter) and bishop (overseer) denote the same function. The first term is borrowed from the synagogue and the second from Greek communities. In later years, one came to emphasize the dignity of the role and the other the duty.

It is this role of elder or bishop that is pertinent to present-day church polity. Elders did not magically appear in the New Testament. "Elders of the people" and "elders of Israel" were associated with Moses and his dealing with the people. They later administered local government in Israel and had a hand in national affairs even after Israel became a monarchy. Elders achieved fresh prominence after the exile and served government functions. The administration and execution of justice often fell to them. They were also involved in conveying the Word of God to the people and in representing the people before God. Other nations had elders as well. In every case, the right to the title was due to maturity (age), esteem in which the individual was held, and experience.

It is only natural, then, that elders appeared in New Testament times as a model for church leadership. Every synagogue was ruled by elders. Elders were charged with carrying forward the work begun by the apostles and their delegates.

Elders were gifted people drawn to the function and not ambitious for the office. Indeed, it was a role and not a position. First Timothy 3:1-10 literally begins with "If anyone oversight aspires to"—if anyone aspires to have oversight. "Aspire" means to stretch out to, to reach forward to, to desire earnestly. It is different from a desire or ambition for office. This is a natural urging to fulfill a function. Based on calling and certain qualifications (1 Timothy 3:1-10, Titus 1:5-9), it appears elders were appointed in two ways. In some cases, the people were involved in the appointment. Acts 14:23 literally says, "And having appointed for them in every church elders." "Having appointed" means to stretch out the hand, to constitute by voting, to appoint. Appointment was done with the involvement and concurrence of the people. This is the same word used in 2 Corinthians 8:19, where again it is clear that the consensus of the people was involved. In selecting elders from among them, Paul seems to have given much weight to the church members' confidence in the appointees.

Titus 1:5-9 illustrates another manner in which elders were appointed. It literally says "and should appoint in each city." "Should appoint" means to place, set, constitute. In the context there appears to be no involvement of the local body, but elders are given their responsibilities based on an evaluation of their qualifications by spiritual leadership.

Historically, three forms of government have grown up around these roles. The hierarchical form of government is one in which bishops govern the church. The federal form of government involves the rule of elders who are given authority by the congregation or by an appointing authority. It is a representative form of government in which the people govern, not directly, but through their representative elders. The congregational form of government allows no man or group to exercise authority over a local assembly, but places the responsibility for government in the hands of the members themselves.

Models of organization came from the environment. The household model, or house church, grew out of the practice of the early church (especially the Pauline groups) to meet in private homes. On the other hand, many of the early churches took on the structure of the voluntary association. The early Roman Empire witnessed a luxuriant growth of clubs, guilds, and associations of all sorts. Many early churches patterned themselves after voluntary associations because this approach was consistent with their social setting and kept them from being labeled as cults, which were regarded as seedbeds of immorality and sedition. Again, the synagogue became a model for many early churches and contributed significantly to the view that Christianity was an offshoot of Judaism. Many early Christians took the synagogue as the nearest and most natural model. Since the synagogue also incorporated elements of the household and voluntary association models, it was easy to export in a form to which most cultures would give legal recognition. Later the philosophic or rhetorical school became a model for the early church. As the apologists came into their own and the Christian church came under scrutiny, the model of a school was pursued quite deliberately to deflect suspicion, combat heresy, and establish credibility.

It is clear that much of how the church was organized and led was determined by social factors. No group can persist for any appreciable time without developing some patterns of leadership, some differentiation of roles among its members, some means of managing conflict, some ways of articulating shared values and norms, and some sanctions to ensure acceptable levels of conformity to those norms. What form of polity or rule was chosen (regardless of model) appears to have been a combination of cultural norms, social necessity, and biblical values. What allowed them to fit into society without violating biblical mandates appears to have been a basic rule of thumb: *Do whatever works without violating Scripture or alienating society*. To apply this rule, they became careful students both of the Word and their world.

Leadership is a shared function within the parameters of the church's organizational structure and polity. Paul describes the Body of Christ in 1 Corinthians 12 in terms of its different parts—like the physical body with its ear, eye, hand, foot, etc.—all equal in importance but different in function. He describes (verse 18) how God has placed each member alongside each other just how He chooses. Then later, Paul begins to list certain roles (verse 28)—apostle, prophet, teachers—that God has appointed. The incorrect assumption is that these people are somehow different than the members mentioned earlier. They are not. These are some of the roles certain members of the Body, at God's choosing and placing, are to serve. The omnicompetent church leader is not pictured here. Rather, leadership in the Body is a plural function, not a singular position.

In Ephesians 4:11-12, Paul describes apostles, prophets, evangelists, and pastor-teachers as people serving in these roles for an express purpose. Equipping the saints, in the sense of the word used, evokes images of a physician resetting a bone or a fisherman cleaning, repairing, and preparing his net for use. These roles, served by a number of people, are designed to maintain the health of the Body for its work or ministry.

Scripture certainly embraces authority in leadership. Military, government, civil, business, and spiritual authority are all part of God's economy. However, the church too easily borrows from the world its model of leadership. The general, politician, or chief executive officer becomes the individualistic pattern for leadership in the Body. But when the disciples argued among themselves regarding who would be the leader when Jesus was gone, He gave a very interesting answer. Jesus reminded them how the world uses authority and stated emphatically, "It shall not be so among you" (Mark 10:43, NKJV). He went on to say that the leader is a servant in the way he uses authority. Whoever in His Kingdom wishes to be first must be a servant of others. Prominence and control cannot be goals! The goal must be to develop gifts in the Body so that the prominent leader becomes unnecessary.

Several years ago, I saw a cartoon that expresses this concept well. Four men approached their pastor stating, "You've done such a good job in discipling the congregation we don't need you anymore." An impossible ideal? Perhaps. But the principle is sound. The responsibility of the leadership is to work themselves out of a job by effectively discipling the members of the local church.

NOTE
1. Charles Colson, *Against the Night* (Ann Arbor, MI: Servant Publications, 1989), page 170.

13

Real Discipleship

W hat does Jesus expect from us as His disciples? The answer we usually hear to that question is *obedience*. Several years ago, a pastor friend told me he always goes for the "jugular" when he counsels. And in response to my question, "What is the jugular?" he responded, "The will." But is it really?

Transformation begins in the mind as we begin to see God's view of life. Obedience is clearly a significant part of growth, but if compliance with God's "rules" is a way of winning His favor, we severely err in our minds, especially if we see His favor as pleasant circumstances. As we saw in John 13-17, doing good in exchange for painfree living is clearly not His way of looking at life.

So many times we look at the heroes of the faith and see appealing blessings. In a quick overview of Hebrews 11 we see Abel, Enoch, Noah, Abraham, and others who received temporal blessings for faith and obedience. But beginning at verse 35, we see quite a different story. For these other heroes of the faith, their faith and obedience brought a radically different consequence:

Others were tortured and refused to be released, so that they might gain a better resurrection. Some faced jeers and flogging, while still others were chained and put in prison. They were stoned; they were sawed in two; they were put to death by the sword. They went about in sheepskins and goatskins, destitute, persecuted and mistrusted—the world was not worthy of them. They wandered in deserts and mountains, and in caves and holes in the ground.

These were all commended for their faith, yet none of them received what had been promised. God had planned something better for us so that only together with us would they be made perfect. (Hebrews 11:35-40)

God's Expectations

My (Bill's) first reaction to this portion of Scripture was, "Why is God so inconsistent?" But if one is committed to the authority of Scripture, that is the wrong question to ask. The question we must ask is, "What is God teaching me through what seems to me an inconsistency?" The fact is that God's view of life this side of Heaven is radically different from ours.

As previous chapters have stated, we will have suffering; absence of suffering is not a reward for faith. God allows suffering to shape and mold us into the image of His Son as a witness to the world for Him. While we are undergoing trials and tribulations, Peter tells us:

Humble yourselves, therefore, under God's mighty hand, that he may lift you up in due time. Cast all your anxiety on him because he cares for you.

Be self-controlled and alert. Your enemy the devil prowls around like a roaring lion looking for someone to devour. Resist him, standing firm in the faith, because you know that your brothers throughout the world are undergoing the same kind of sufferings.

And the God of all grace, who called you to his eternal glory in Christ, after you have suffered for a little while, will himself restore you and make you strong, firm and steadfast. (1 Peter 5:6-10)

He will restore, strengthen, and convict you of the relevance of His truth to life. This is what we have been called to. Peter calls us to endure hardship and harsh treatment, responding to it as Christ responded to unfair treatment: "leaving you an example, that you should follow in his steps" (1 Peter 2:18-21).

This is the core of our ministry as believers: to respond uniquely to the circumstances that He has allowed us to face as a testimony to who He is. Each one of us has a general call and a unique situation in which we are to be His disciples.

Sphere of Ministry

Everyone has a sphere of ministry. That may sound like a strange term, but we all have one. Paul talked about sphere of ministry in 2 Corinthians 10:13-16. The idea is one of God-appointed boundaries, limits to a range of action or duty. Paul describes his field in Romans 15:11-21 as being the Gentiles at large. We know from Scripture that others had different spheres of service. Peter seemed primarily focused on Jews. Titus and Timothy took special assignments primarily among Gentiles. Apollos confounded Jews in the synagogues but ministered to Gentiles also. The Apostle John's sphere seemed more functional, serving as a father to all. Barnabas had a ministry of encouragement that went beyond political and racial boundaries.

Part of what provides people-limits to our ministry is our spiritual gifting. Paul describes in 1 Corinthians 12 how the Spirit has given each believer a giftedness determined by His choice (verse 11). Each gifted believer is placed in the Body of

Christ just where God wants (verse 18). The ministries of Paul and Apollos illustrate this unique enabling and placement for ministry (1 Corinthians 3). One planted while the other watered; each was a servant performing the tasks God assigned (3:5-6).

How much help do we provide believers in understanding their God-given design? How much freedom do we exercise in enabling and encouraging people to operate in the context of that design? Often, we try to fit people into the mold of our ministry program, regardless of gifting, experience, maturity, or even desires.

I (Jeff) consulted with one Christian organization experiencing difficult times for just this reason. They were suffering an exodus of personnel that portended worse things to come. What was happening? This organization had a methodical approach to ministry. Only those who preferred to operate in a structured environment seemed to flourish. Others felt discouraged, bound by the mandate to maintain conformity. Those with a need to innovate felt out of place.

Since this ministry specialized in developing curriculum, training leaders, and providing educational resources, most of the employees had gifts related to teaching. However, employees with very different gifts—even those who preferred control-oriented ministry and operated best with clearly defined programs—found themselves uncomfortable also. Many of the staff had gone to work for this organization right out of college. Now, years later, they had enough of life under their belt to understand experientially that their design and desires were not a good fit in their work experience anymore. So, they left.

This was unfortunate. The audience this ministry focused on was changing also. Their results in ministry were falling off as their work related less and less to the needs of the audience. The very people leaving were the ones needed to help with the problem. The Body of Christ, in any expression, needs a spectrum of active gifts in order to be healthy. This organization needed the creative talent of those departing to help it shift into a posture of relevance for current and future audiences. It was in serious need of large-scale organizational change. Without change, it was doomed to a slow, and therefore relatively unnoticed, decline. To stave off the flow of needed resources out of the organization, outside intervention was required.

But what does outside intervention mean? Clearly, the work of the Spirit of God is necessary, but He works through men and women as they study and apply God's truth. What is man's job and where does his responsibility end?

Man's Job, God's Job

Brothers, I could not address you as spiritual but as worldly—mere infants in Christ. I gave you milk, not solid food, for you were not yet ready for it. Indeed you are still not ready. You are still worldly. For since there is jealousy and quarreling among you, are you not worldly? Are you not acting like mere men? For when one says, "I follow Paul," and another, "I follow Apollos," are you not mere men?

What, after all, is Apollos? And what is Paul? Only servants, through whom you came to believe—as the Lord has assigned to each his task. I planted the seed, Apollos watered it, but *God made it grow*. So neither he who plants nor he who waters is anything, but only God who makes things grow. The man who plants and the man who waters have one purpose, and each will be rewarded according to his own labor. For we are God's fellow workers; you are God's field, God's building. (1 Corinthians 3:1-9, emphasis mine)

Why did Paul accuse the Corinthian believers of being worldly? Because they were clinging to the ways of man and not

164 / *The Dynamics of Change*

the ways of God. I (Bill) don't think it would be stretching the truth to say that a major aspect of what Paul was condemning was looking to men to find formulas for growth rather than promoting faithfulness and allowing God to produce the growth.

Our job is faithfulness, personal growth, and proclamation of His truth through discipleship, growth in Christlikeness, and evangelism. We must trust the results to Him. We must see Him as the change agent or we will continually face growing frustration as we don't achieve the results we want in our time frame.

When we see this truth that God is in charge of blessing our efforts, then we find a freedom to initiate, innovate, and fail without being a failure. As we initiate and innovate, what should be our core direction?

God's Commission and Commandment

It may seem through all of this that we have a negative view of the local church. Not at all. In fact, I (Jeff) am very optimistic about the prospects for the local church. However, I am also realistic that we as a church are in trouble. Not enough trouble yet for our own constituency to notice, but sufficient trouble for overall church growth in America to be at a standstill. For every growing church, there are several shrinking ones on the local scene. Yet I see no alternative on the horizon. The local church continues to be a primary manifestation of the activities of the Body of Christ in this country. The implication is that the Western tradition of what it means to be a local body of believers is going to have to change. Business as usual just won't face the challenge of our culture!

In anticipation of change, let me suggest a neglected balance. Christ's Great Commission (Matthew 28:18-20) must be balanced with an equal focus on Christ's Great Commandment (John 13:34-35). Many churches can articulate a mission philosophy and can showcase ministry programs. How many can showcase a radical perspective regarding body life: ministry that touches common longings in relevant, uncompromising ways? Where are the programs, services, and resources that enable the ordinary man or woman to feel his own longings sufficiently to be able to touch others with a supernaturally learned love? Relationship—community in the biblical sense—will impact the world as it affirms and demonstrates the proclamations of the church. People need to see us living our message.

To focus solely on the Great Commission is to produce sterile ministry. To focus solely on the Great Commandment will dilute ministry effort and reduce outreach to those in reach of "holy huddles." Both must be held in active tension if the church is to grow in its inward maturity as well as its outward influence.

As we properly balance ministry between the Great Commandment and the Great Commission and see God as the One who provides growth, we then begin to limit our responsibility to faithfulness, not results. This is the beginning of true freedom and peace in the midst of adverse circumstances.

14

The Church Rekindled

M ost people I (Bill) know feel trapped and disappointed. Some suffer with the financial pressure of supporting several children through college. Others are married to someone they no longer like but see no "biblical" way to end the marriage. Most of us have cried out to God, but He seems to remain silent. There is no clear way to resolve our situations. So we ask, "Where is the freedom promised in Scripture?"

Much of our feeling of being trapped flows from an unbiblical definition of what freedom really is. I tend to think of freedom as possessing enough money so I don't have to go to work anymore, so that I can pursue the "good" life. As a result, I become a slave of the desire to be "free" and, as many people do, pursue it to the grave unless I seek God's perspective on freedom.

True Freedom
The writer of Hebrews has this to say about freedom in Christ:

> Let us throw off everything that hinders and the sin that
> so easily entangles, and let us run with perseverance

the race marked out for us. Let us fix our eyes on Jesus,
the author and perfecter of our faith, who for the joy
set before him endured the cross, scorning its shame,
and sat down at the right hand of the throne of God.
Consider him who endured such opposition from sinful
men, so that you will not grow weary and lose heart.
(Hebrews 12:1-3)

Several important facts stand out from this passage. First, we
must throw off anything that entangles us so that we are free to
live according to God's guidelines. Anything that hinders this
direction is sin. That includes false views of how to live and
what is important. Second, what is most important is that we
fix our eyes on Jesus and His example.

I recently heard my father, Larry Crabb, Sr., speak on what
is important to him as a man of seventy-eight years. He commented on a "scholarly" book he had read on the subject of
law and grace, two leading schools of theological thought, and
the proper position between the two. My father commented,
"As I age, this type of writing becomes painfully boring to
me," even though "it used to fascinate me. . . . The sad thing is
that doctrines, proof of my position, impressing others becomes
all-important and I lose the GLOW of all that Christ is."

Certainly correct doctrine is vital. But becoming an accurate technician of Scripture may hinder me from fixing my eyes
on Jesus. Larry Crabb, Jr. has stated, "We may know the facts
of Scripture, but too often we miss its message." That message
is to model Christ to our families, church members (even those
with whom we disagree), and the world around us.

Some of the encumbrances we must lay aside in order to
find freedom in Christ may be the traditions and beliefs that are
hindering us from fixing our eyes on Christ. This is a potentially
dangerous statement! Because many have compromised truth,
the core doctrines of Scripture concerning God's sovereignty,

Christ's deity, and His death, burial, and resurrection have lost their authority. So we do have to make sure that we don't compromise Scripture while we are re-evaluating our traditions, beliefs, and methods. But the *fear* of compromise must not keep us from that re-evaluation.

One encumbrance is a false view of what my responsibility is. As we saw in chapters 9 and 13, I am not responsible for results, only for running the race with perseverance. This fact gives me the freedom to try and fail.

Freedom to Fail

At the time of Christ, His death appeared to be a failure, the end of a dream. But what looked to men like failure was a resounding success for God. When we see that principle, freedom can be a reality for us. We can become free to be visionaries, to initiate, to innovate, to fail (not see desired results) and grow personally. Throughout this book we have told story after story about people trapped by their traditions, social bias, cultural hang-ups, and more. As they seek to be obedient to God's call to the church, some will break out of molds of irrelevancy. But doing so will create a huge possibility of failure. But more importantly, it will create new freedom. The examples we've cited of people and institutions concerned with redemptive relevance among their own constituency as well as among the lost have not grown without difficulty and struggle.

How can we reach the Sams, Bills, Gingers, and others we described in the opening chapters of this book? Some are completely removed even from Christian terminology. Others are believers with false expectations of their union with Christ; they think life should now "work better" in the sense of being easier. Are we responsible for their well-being and for "meeting their needs," or are we responsible to contextualize the gospel so that it is relevant to their situation, even if it's not what they want to hear?

Responsibility to Rekindle

When I (Jeff) was a child, I spent a great deal of time playing. The kids in my neighborhood would play cowboys and Indians, doctor, house, or other roles. We would emulate what we saw modeled in the media or by our parents without ever questioning the relevance of the role. I don't think any of us grew up to be cowboys or Indians, but we did become doctors, mechanics, lawyers, teachers, nurses, carpenters, engineers, sales people, secretaries, and so on. Adulthood forced upon us some realizations. What, really, is a teacher? Is what I grew up believing about teachers true? Is what I understand about teaching relevant and needed for the students of today? At some point in our lives, most of us—directly or indirectly—began to address the questions of relevance. We quit playing and started to face life as it really is.

If the American church is to be rekindled, it must repent and change. We must ask, "Are our ministries just keeping us busy, or are we really equipping saints for the work of service (Ephesians 4:12)?" If Jesus left the church in the world for the sake of the lost, why do we consume most of the resources of the church on ourselves? It is too easy to justify ourselves (Luke 16:15). But in reality, we have become our own subculture, socially isolated from those in the world we have been commissioned to influence. (In fact, the world, which doesn't even believe in absolute truth, may be influencing the church more than the reverse.)

Reflecting upon the growing irrelevance of some ministries even to those within our congregations, my neighbor remarked, "Our church has some good things for the children [day care], but there is nothing for me personally." It is easy to say, "You're just feeling sorry for yourself. Get busy and involved," without taking his question seriously and asking why church doesn't seem relevant. We must become a radical subculture modeling Christian love. But that will mean ceasing to be a Laodicean church whose heart is barely distinguishable from the world's.

We must get in touch with reality and not assume, as we did when we were children, that everything our predecessors did is right for our times. Each generation must own and contextualize the gospel for itself, convinced that cultures change but Scripture is relevant to all cultures.

The key to contextualization for this generation is the ordinary person—the laity, not the clergy. Motivating, mobilizing, enabling, and facilitating the laity in ministry—not merely compliance to the pastor's agenda—must take place if the church is to be rekindled.

We must move from counting our successes in terms of membership, baptisms, converts, filled parking spaces, etc. to evaluating the process of spiritual maturity. Attitude is more important than attainment. Faithfulness is greater than measured progress in a program. Why are these distinctions important? Because as organizations, we tend to define too rigidly, while as a movement in God's Kingdom, we need to describe processes, not measure products. As a church, we have defined body life, for example, in terms of a congregation (the meeting of a group of people in a building). Yet the Bible describes body life as community, as believers in the world but not of it. Which did Jesus do in Scripture? Did He define, or did He describe? Was He concerned with attainment, or with attitudes of the inner heart? Will He pour out His Spirit on programs or on people earnestly seeking Him?

A disciple is a learner, a follower. Captured in the word is the idea of thought accompanied by action. To be someone's follower in this sense is more than an intellectual assent or an academic pursuit. It is the pursuit of everything another Person represents to the point of fundamental life change. In the New Testament, men and women are called disciples of Jesus, even before conversion. Even mature followers, years after conversion, are called His disciples. The picture of discipleship is one of a process where progress is toward relationship with Christ or maturity in Christ. You can be a disciple and not be a Christian. Sadly, you can be a Christian and not be a disciple. We must be about discipleship, a change in heart attitude based on the relevance of Scripture to life that results in lasting behavior change.

A New Philosophy

My neighbor was essentially asking, "What's in it for me?" The church needs to ask, "How can I bridge to the person asking that question, and then move him on to the right questions?" Traditionally, we tell those coming to the church, "Here is everything you need to know." But a philosophy of contextualization doesn't merely provide information. It looks for where Scripture can be brought to bear on the real issues and what applications real need suggests. These applications abound in a society that is deteriorating because it has disregarded the Judeo-Christian value system.

Change is constant in society, sometimes imperceptibly slow, sometimes overwhelmingly swift. The church must adjust to reality in its ministries if it is to regain relevance. What will attract and retain constituents is not a big name or a well-advertised program. Only ministry that is plainly relevant to life issues and of true value will bring and hold new life in the church.

Many, like my neighbor, are returning to church because they have become parents. They are realizing that children need a source of values. Neighborhoods, school, and family are not providing values adequately, so many people are taking another look at the church.

But we tend to capitalize on this opportunity for meaningful ministry out of an old way of thinking: bigger is better. A leading church growth organization sells its services based on marketplace principles and their application to evaluating "markets" of churchgoers like my neighbor. This packaging of ministry may accommodate some social realities, but it ignores biblical ones. To understand the audience's norms and values is not the same thing as a market analysis of potential clients.

Some experts appear to believe that the important principle in stimulating church growth is making sure the parking lot is big enough. They judge a minister's success by whether people keep coming and giving. But such ideas about growth inhibit contextualization. It is God who gives growth.

Ministry to the Body and the lost must be contextualized. This may mean eliminating certain methods, traditions, habits, or ways of thinking that obscure the message of the church to its intended audience. Roles and functions in the church should reflect gifts, calling, desires, talents, and so on—not the expediency of filling a need with a warm body, maintaining fiscal growth, or financing the latest program. Maintaining church functions should not absorb resources so much that the Body fails to enter the lost community meaningfully and redemptively.

If we are to change, we must face the truth regarding the church's needs today. Leadership in the church is a function, not a position or office. Consider 1 Timothy 3:1, "If anyone sets his heart on being an overseer, he desires a noble task." Most English translations use the word *office* to describe the role of overseer, but it does not appear in the Greek. A literal rendition is, "Faithful is the word if anyone oversight aspires to a good work he desires." When we make "a good work" into a position or office rather than a role or function, we are succumbing to cultural values—the pride of position, the love of professionalism—rather than to biblical teaching. The church is intended to be a polity by consent: Its members are members voluntarily, and no one's interests (except God's) outweigh anyone else's. Therefore, we must exercise the art of leadership amid the brokering of everyone's interests, the weak as well as the powerful.

Movement can be contributed to, participated in, but not controlled. The church needs to be part of a movement, not an institution. Institutions tend not to be in touch with the realities of now; movements, by definition, cope with the realities of the times. Therefore, if the church is to be rekindled as a movement, we must motivate and mobilize a laity in touch with the world they live among. And a biblically contextualized ministry will be found in a movement in which the Great Commandment shares equal importance and application with the Great Commission.

Living with Reality

There is no formula for successfully controlling the actions of another, even if it is genuinely in his best interest. God sometimes responds to faithfulness with a visible blessing, such as numerical growth or a changed son or daughter. But other faithful men and women will cry out like Jeremiah, "Why is my pain unending and my wound grievous and incurable?" (Jeremiah 15:18). The heroes of the faith in Hebrews 11 came to radically different ends. Some were blessed during their lifetimes on earth; others were tortured and killed for their faith. Were the latter less faithful? The answer is a resounding "No!"

Our sovereign God will not let us cling to programs for success. We would then look to methods and not to Jesus Christ. The potential leader must emulate Christ above all else and accept no responsibility beyond what God has given him.

Responsibility of Leadership

Leadership is far more than getting people in line. If we were able to get people in line to make us prominent, we would tend to become puffed up, thinking that our efforts were something in themselves and that the power of God's Spirit was less than all in all.

When I dwell on John 13–17 as Christ's manual for His leaders, I feel frustrated, confused, and dependent: frustrated because it's not a "how-to-do-it" procedure; confused because the only really clear teaching is to model Christlike character while suffering, for there is no easy way out of suffering until Christ returns; and dependent because I don't have any real power in myself. If God had written a step-by-step "how-to-do-it" book, I would have a false sense of control. "I can make it happen!" But I can't. Only He can.

If God didn't write that kind of instruction manual, how can we as men write one? And if we could, how would we measure success? Only by visible, measurable, empirical results. But God looks at the heart, something we can see only evidences of—evidences that may or may not reflect reality. Numerical growth may or may not reflect personal growth. An apparent disciple may not even be a Christian.

The greatest challenge of leadership is not to manipulate people to follow, but to grow personally in Christ, so that what God highly esteems is also what we highly esteem and model to our families, church members, and the general public.

This challenge of personal growth is preeminent. But a second challenge is to innovate, contextualize, and initiate, to take risks, knowing that what may look like failure to us may help us grow in active dependence and may later be used by God in visible impact. Pastors must know the real issues with which their people struggle.

I recently polled a class of singles, ages twenty-five to forty, asking, "What are your questions about life that you feel the church is not helping you deal with?" They responded with six typed pages of questions on parenting, singleness, why people struggle, and so on—all questions that can be taken to the Bible for priceless insights. The Bible is sufficient to face the issues of any culture at any time in history. It was penned in a culture, but as the Word of God, it is not limited by culture.

Therefore, instead of delivering a fixed agenda, our teaching can and must address the burning questions of our culture and congregations.

A major part of innovation, contextualization, and initiation is to orchestrate gifts and develop community. A strong preacher may bring people in the front door, but without community, they will soon be out the back door. Community means sharing responsibility, developing gifts, and becoming a place of refuge and hope in a culture that has no hope to offer other than "go for it"—a self-centered approach to life that is destroying its followers.

Biblical methods and emphases may differ radically among yuppie, blue collar, and ethnic communities, but the core message of John 13–17 applies to all. We must make truth relevant because it is relevant. Regardless of circumstances, if it is genuinely God's truth and not the traditions of men "supported" by Scriptures, it is relevant.

Our third challenge is faithfulness. If our efforts seem to fail, we need to look to the examples of Scripture, where we find men and women whose faithfulness didn't produce visible results until after their sometimes painful deaths. A major aspect of faithfulness is trusting God for the results.

> What, after all, is Apollos? And what is Paul? Only servants, through whom you came to believe—as the Lord has assigned to each his task. I planted the seed, Apollos watered it, but God made it grow. So neither he who plants nor he who waters is anything, but only God who makes things grow. (1 Corinthians 3:5-7)

Our challenge is to plant and water in a culturally relevant, thoroughly biblical way. His job is to bless in His way and on His schedule.

Foundations for the Future

Martin Lloyd-Jones writes, "We see the Christian church . . . ineffective in a world of sin and shame, a world in which is increasingly manifesting in a horrifying manner, Godlessness and hatred or antagonism to God. There is only one hope for such a world, and that is a revived church."[1]

He goes on: "You can not get a revival whenever you want or just work one up. It is wrong to say that if you fulfill certain conditions, or do certain things a revival will come."[2] We are powerless. Any revival of the church's impact, such as occurred at Pentecost, is beyond our control. But in order to gain a false sense of control, we organize, institutionalize, and establish programs. Lloyd-Jones comments,

> I am certain that the world outside is not going to pay much attention to all the organized efforts of the Christian church. The one thing she will pay attention to is a body filled with the spirit of rejoicing. That is how Christianity conquered the ancient world. It was the amazing joy of these people. Even when you threw them in prison, or even to death, it did not matter, they went on rejoicing; rejoicing in tribulation.[3]

What he is speaking of is rare today. In our technological world of instant everything, we don't like or understand Romans 5:3-5 and other passages that show God using tribulation to gradually develop character. But with the radical shift of our culture in the last fifty years, tribulation, not prosperity, may soon be in store for followers of Christ. What we stand for is slowly and systematically being made illegal. To face the possibility of persecution, we must take the words of our Lord in John 13-17 seriously.

To face the future, we must look to the past—to Christ's preparation of His disciples, and to the early church that met daily in homes for teaching of the apostles' doctrine, fellow-ship, worship, and prayer. Certainly there were leaders, but the emphasis of Acts 2 was community, dynamic community in which all the people were involved and focused on the person and work of Jesus Christ. Contrast the present, where too often the focus is on the man in the pulpit, lecture-oriented programs, and meeting congregational "needs."

I wonder how the members of the early church viewed their "needs" when they were being persecuted or killed. They had a focus that we have lost today, a focus that we can regain only by an outpouring of God's Spirit, perhaps even through persecution. We need to be driven to the basics of Christianity: we have died with Christ, and death for the Christian is merely changing realms. This fact is the basis for Paul's statement:

> I consider that our present sufferings are not worth com-paring with the glory that will be revealed in us. . . . For I am convinced that neither death nor life, neither angels nor demons, neither the present nor the future, nor any powers, neither height nor depth, nor anything else in creation, will be able to separate us from the love of God that is in Christ Jesus our Lord. (Romans 8:18,38-39)

The foundations for the future are seen only in the roots of the past: men and women facing the reality of life in deep community under the authority of Scripture. May we become a praying, caring community so that the world of the twenty-first century may see Christ as we respond to our Lord's command and prayer:

> A new command I give to you: Love one another. As I have loved you, so you must love one another. By this all men will know that you are my disciples, if you love one another. (John 13:34-35)

I have given them the glory that you gave me, that they may be one as we are one: I in them and you in me. *May they be brought to complete unity to let the world know that you sent me and have loved them even as you have loved me.* (John 17:22-23, emphasis mine)

May we diligently work to fulfill both the Great Commission and the Great Commandment, so that God's truth becomes relevant to His own and a powerful testimony to the world of the person and work of Jesus Christ.

NOTES

1. Martin Lloyd-Jones, *Joy Unspeakable* (Wheaton, IL: Harold Shaw Publishers, 1984), page 33.
2. Lloyd-Jones, page 52.
3. Lloyd-Jones, page 102.